O12

FASCISM AS A MASS MOVEMENT

FASCISM
as a mass movement

Mihaly Vajda

Allison & Busby, London

First published in Great Britain by
Allison and Busby Limited
6a Noel Street, London W1V 3RB

Copyright © Mihaly Vajda 1976
(Parts of the work were originally published by
Magyar Filozofiai Szemle in 1970 and *Törtenelmi Szemle* in 1972)

Translation copyright © Allison & Busby 1976

ISBN 0 85031 176 4 (hardback)
ISBN 0 85031 177 2 (paperback)

Set in 11pt Lectura and printed by
Villiers Publications Ltd, Ingestre Road, London NW5 1UL

CONTENTS

FOREWORD

This book is not a "historical" study in the proper sense of the term. It is not a description of "what happened". It does not provide a chronicle of the fascist movements nor of the various fascist dictatorships. It is, rather, a historiosophical attempt to find out the *meaning* of what happened, and what the relevance of fascism is (both as a movement and as a political form of rule) to the history of "civil society". It is an attempt to take cognizance of a phenomenon which, though short-lived, was an acting protagonist on the twentieth-century historical scene, and with this to gain a deeper insight into the essence of "civil society" itself and the "political state" that goes with it. The analysis necessarily follows what looks like reverse order. It sets out from the nature of "civil society" and the "political state" and Marx's analysis of these complexes, and goes on to elucidate the content and functions of fascism. But the analysis will only have reached its real "secret" purpose if the meaning of fascism as revealed here sheds new light on the world-historical epoch which produced this freak phenomenon in the first place, and which provided me with the basis for my attempt to make the phenomenon understandable.

I stand by the basic viewpoints of this study and nearly all the details (it was written during 1969 and 1970), even if I do not always stand by the way they are formulated; otherwise I would not have consented to its publication. However, there is one essential part of my original theoretical standpoint which has undergone a certain change.

At the time of writing, my views of philosophy and social theory remained essentially under the influence of Georg Lukács's *History and Class Consciousness*.[1] I accepted the basic idea of Lukács's work, i.e. that there is a distinction between "empirical" and "imputed" class consciousness, and that the *actual* consciousness of individuals belonging to a certain class which becomes manifest through their actions is not the same as the class consciousness which the individuals of the class in question *ought* to

7

possess as an inevitable consequence of their class affiliation. This kind of opposition between actual class consciousness and behaviour on the one hand, and class affiliation and class consciousness as logically construed on the other, led to certain simplifications. Sometimes I could only reconcile them with the real social and political processes by using the most elaborate kinds of theoretical construction. I do not have the room here to try and analyse the problems involved in this. Lukács's ideas cannot be transcended without a critical reconsideration of Marx's concept of class.

I shall simply point out to the reader two aspects which have played a substantial role in my study. First of all, Lukács's ideas cannot provide the basis for explaining why a "revolutionary situation" is not born unconditionally out of every single "crisis situation". Why does the proletariat not acquire, in every instance of deep-going social, economic and political crisis, the "imputed" proletarian class consciousness which is alleged to be a logical consequence of the essence of its class position? I emphasise repeatedly in my book that fascism is the offspring of a situation pregnant with crisis but not with revolution. How and why a situation like this can come about is something which remains unaccounted for in my book, or rather I try to explain it by the failure of earlier revolutionary aspirations (which is just as much of a non-explanation, in the light of the ideas mentioned above).

The second aspect concerns one of the most fundamental and polemically formulated theses in my book. This is my statement that on the one hand fascism can only be accounted for if it is treated as a phenomenon of capitalist society, but that on the other hand it cannot be regarded as a movement which is actually launched by the ruling class, and that moreover it openly contradicts the interests of the ruling class in certain cases. I stress that this contradiction occurs because the ideology and organisational forms of the fascist movement are deeply rooted in "petty bourgeois" attitudes. But when this idea is linked to the concept of class which I referred to above, the implication is that bourgeois society is divided into three classes. The bourgeoisie is apparently interested in the transition to the neo-capitalist system (when the intensive phase of capitalism is reached), the proletariat is interested in creating the classless society, and the petty bourgeoisie in between is prepared to "accept" both: but if the concrete

8

historical situation excludes both the first and the second solution, then the petty bourgeoisie necessarily becomes fascist. It was, among other reasons, the fact that I could only transplant the Lukácsian concept into the concrete historical context by means of extremely elaborate theoretical constructions that convinced me, after having finished the book, that Lukács's concept of class-consciousness and the underlying simplified class analysis of "bourgeois" society are untenable.

The problems which concern the concept of "nation" are only indirectly connected with all this. But they exist all the same. I still regard what I said in my book about the national character of fascist movements as valid. But it is my current belief that a theoretical advance is necessary in this area too, if we are to grasp the fascist phenomenon in such a way as to deepen our understanding of the bourgeois world-epoch.

M.V.
Budapest, January 1976

THE CLASS ORGANISATION OF THE PETTY BOURGEOISIE

I Fascist Dictatorship

The definitive character of fascist dictatorship is that it sprang from a *mass movement* and, as a capitalist form of rule, depended on this movement for support. It was the leaders and participants of the movement, not bourgeois politicians, who assumed the power functions of the dictatorship. My approach will undoubtedly seem somewhat arbitrary in its methodology. There is a widespread view that every anti-democratic form of capitalist rule after the first world war must be regarded as fascist, and so one might expect it necessary to prove that the Italian and German dictatorships where characterised by different traits from those of all other dictatorships at the time, in order subsequently to ascribe any importance at all to the fascist *movement* itself. But I consider this arbitrariness to be admissible, since I have deliberately chosen to base my analysis on the standpoint of the revolutionary workers' movement. And in this respect there can be no doubt that régimes such as the Horthy dictatorship in Hungary were fundamentally different from fascist and national socialist rule.

It is true, of course, that the Horthy régime was preceded by the period of white terror, when the outrages of the counter-revolutionary commandos disregarded even the appearance of legality. But it was different inasmuch as this white terror was the reaction to a defeated revolution, a fallen revolutionary power; and it must be remembered that this transitional phase was followed by one of consolidation, in which the traditional ruling classes exercised direct political power — which was not the case in Italy and Germany. Moreover, from my chosen standpoint it is of crucial importance that this rule was exercised in such a way that a certain degree of freedom was granted to the labour movement, if not to its revolutionary forms. The Social Democratic Party existed in Hungary and was far from unimportant, the trade unions functioned; during the consolidation period, the anti-communist terror was conducted by lawful police and legislative means.

It can be argued that régimes like that of Horthy gradually borrow traits from fascist dictatorships. In Hungary, for example, anti-semitism became official from the mid-1930s onwards. But this did not mean the wholesale adoption of fascist methods, since the aim was not to satisfy mass demands — not that the traditional ruling strata would have been willing to adopt them, for they dreaded any kind of mass movement. What happened in Hungary was an acquiescence in certain principles of the fascist régimes (particularly the nazi one) which had become allies. These principles partly corresponded to the desires of the traditional ruling strata themselves, but were mostly the result of direct or indirect pressure from allied fascist Germany.

The same situation occurred in many other non-democratic European states. I fully agree with Otto Bauer:

> "The 1918 revolution was followed by a counter-revolution. But this counter-revolution did not display fascist characteristics everywhere. Poland's democracy was followed by the military dictatorship of Pilsudski. In Yugoslavia, democracy was replaced by old-style dynastic military absolutism. The new form of tyranny was first victorious in Italy and Germany. Today, of course, it is the newly discovered form of capitalist dictatorship, the methods of which are imitated by counter-revolutionary governments of a different origin too."[2]

Clara Zetkin put forward a similar view as early as 1923.

Certain aspects of fascism's principles and methods were adopted by numerous other types of dictatorship, and most clearly by Franco in Spain. The Franco régime too, however, cannot be regarded as an example of fascism. I cannot discuss the problem in detail here, but in order to back up my statement I wish to point out the following. First of all, the Spanish dictatorship did not bar the traditional ruling strata from exercising political power. Secondly, it was not forced to even appear to satisfy radical mass demands, since it did not come to power as a mass movement applying pseudo-revolutionary tactics but as an open adversary of revolutionary power, a counter-revolution. Thirdly, it did not have the aggressiveness in foreign policy of the fascist régimes. Finally, and most importantly, it did not carry out the economic function which is characteristic of the fascist system: it did not foster the development of the forces of production but quite definitely hindered it. This is demonstrated all the more clearly by the fact that when Spain did begin to develop economically in the 1960s, so the face of the régime began to change in many ways.

The classic fascist dictatorships are those in which power is exercised by the party, or its leadership, in close conjunction with the stormtroopers' organisation, the latter having developed into a movement. Before seizing power this movement launches organised attacks on working-class organisations; its strength increases in the course of these struggles to the point where it is able to take over the state apparatus without entering into an actual alliance with the traditional ruling strata. This does not mean, of course, that the fascist movement can seize power without the support of those strata. Only the tacit support of the existing régime enables it to violate the rules of the existing legal order in its attacks on working-class organisations. But as soon as the movement has the state apparatus within its grasp, the seizure of power seems — despite the attempt to keep up the appearances of legality — to be a revolutionary transformation. In both the Italian and the German cases, a fascist élite drove the traditional ruling classes out of the direct exercise of political power and did not allow them to organise in opposition. It was only able to create an appearance of complete national integration by eliminating *all* the traditional parties and organisations.

The creation of this system demanded a party which from the beginning would take a stand against "particular" interests within the nation, attacking the "egoism" of both bourgeoisie and proletariat. The party attacked "plutocracy", bolshevism and reformist marxism in equal measure. From its own point of view it was undoubtedly justified in opposing the reformist movements, since reformism (in contrast with the revolutionary socialist movement's aim of creating a society in which the contradictory interests of particular strata no longer exist, for reasons of principle) represents the egoistic interests of the proletariat. By abandoning the aim of a communist transformation of society and fighting only to satisfy the working class's needs within the existing system, it is in fact seeking to assert the interests of one stratum, which necessarily remains particular, against the interests of other particular strata.

15

II The "Totality" Principle as the Ideological Basis of the Fascist Movement

When a fascist dictatorship thus eliminates all the traditional parties (together with their characteristic function of representing the interests of particular social strata) and establishes its own rule, which represents the "total" nation, it is acting in consistency with the spirit of fascist ideology. Theoreticians and historians of fascism have maintained on the most diverse grounds that fascism had no ideology at all, because tactics prevailed and relegated all other elements (including the ideological ones) to the background. But this is to confuse the *ideology* of fascism with the *programmes* of the fascist parties. Of course fascism never hesitated to modify its declared programme in the most radical way, even to reverse it completely if its power interests demanded such a tactic. But it never renounced its own ideology.

It is the common characteristic of every expressly fascist movement that it considers its directly antagonistic ideology to be that which has the purest appeal to particularity, i.e. liberalism and the "rationalism" of liberalism. In Herbert Marcuse's study of fascism he points out that "the struggle first began far from the political arena, as a philosophical controversy with the rationalism, individualism and materialism of the nineteenth century",[3] and in this respect "even marxism appeared [to the fascist ideology] as constantly following liberalism, as its heir and partner".[4] Liberalism (together with the social democratic variety of marxism, which has undoubtedly become a type of liberalism) is, like the rationalism built on particularity, the antagonist of fascism and of fascist ideology. The fundamental and characteristic intention of every genuinely liberal ideology is to create a rational unity of opposing particular interests; and reformist marxism interprets this by regarding the working class as an independent and particular social force, and seeks to create the *kind* of unity of interests in which the interests of this specific class would be met, alongside those of others. Fascist ideology, on the other hand, means the radical negation of particularity, the subordina-

16

tion of every kind of particularity to the "total", "natural-organic" whole, "the nation".

This irrational totality is simply the reverse side of the rational particularity of liberalism. The irrationality of the "totality" has always complemented the one-sided and over-stretched rationality of bourgeois thinking. To put it another way, it is the standpoint of totality which always introduces, explicitly or implicitly, the aspect of irrationality into bourgeois thinking. (This structure of bourgeois thinking and its connection with the structure of bourgeois society was first pointed out, following Marx but using some of Max Weber's ideas, by Georg Lukács.[5] Marcuse's ideas here obviously draw on the study which Lukács made.)

The "vital" element of liberalism is "the optimistic faith in the ultimate victory of reason, which will realise itself above all conflicts of interests and opinion in the harmony of the whole".[6] This rationalism is rooted in the "rationality" of fully developed capitalist commodity production, to which the rationality of the legal regulation of social relations corresponds:

> "The rationalisation of law and the rationalisation of the enterprise (the elements demonstrated by Max Weber to be decisive for the spirit of Western capitalism) are realised to a previously unknown extent. But at this very point liberalist rationalism comes up against barriers that it can no longer surmount of itself. Irrationalist elements seep into it and explode its theoretical conception."[7]

The "whole itself is outside the sphere of rationalisation"[8] and therefore even theoretically "the structure and order of the whole" are "ultimately left to irrational forces: an accidental 'harmony', a 'natural balance' ".[9] With the intensification of class antagonisms and the crisis of classical capitalism, accompanied by repeated collapses of "harmony", these irrational aspects of bourgeois thinking necessarily come to the fore.

Marcuse correctly saw the crisis of liberalism of the classic type. But his prediction that "the total-authoritarian state brings with it the organisation and theory of society that correspond to the monopolistic stage of capitalism"[10] did not prove to be true. The stable organisation of modern monopoly capital has been achieved in the form of manipulated democracy, and modern

17

positivism represents the theory which corresponds to this. Capitalism has only been able to stabilise itself by attempting to satisfy the particular needs of *all* strata (stability is always upset when for some reason or other capitalism does not succeed in achieving this all-embracing satisfaction), and not by an illusory transcendence of particular interests in general. Since Marcuse considered fascism to be the only adequate political form of modern monopoly capitalism, he was also wrong in his assessment of the developmental trends of bourgeois thinking: he regarded irrationalism as the most characteristic tendency of bourgeois thinking in modern capitalism. In the fascist era Marcuse was not the only one to put forward this idea. The same view of the basic developmental trends of capitalism was put forward by Pál Justus in *The Path of Socialism: the New Conditions of Class War* [translation of Hungarian title], and the same view of the development of bourgeois thinking by Georg Lukács in *The Destruction of Reason*, where he regards the contradiction between rationalism and irrationalism as the watershed between the progressive and the reactionary in modern thought.

I believe, however, that we are not faced here with a simple error but with an "ideologically shaped" attitude determined by the real demarcation lines of that historical period. I say "ideologically shaped" because this attitude, in spite of the fact that it *corresponded* to the fundamental interests of the movement, led to unacceptable concessions to bourgeois rationalism. Among other things, it led the theoreticians to neglect the previously well-recognised and basic fact that rationalism and irrationalism were two mutually complementary sides of bourgeois thinking. This trend was very conspicuous in some of Lukács's writings in the forties and fifties: the attacks made on him by official marxists in this period do not alter the fact that his thinking at that time came close in many ways to the hyper-rationalism of the "diamat" conception. Karl Korsch was not forced to make theoretical concessions of this kind, and he rejected the concept of "anti-fascism"; however, during his last years he was no longer capable of exerting any major ideological influence on the left-wing movements. During the rise and power of fascism, it was absolutely clear that, as far as the revolutionary mission and project of the proletariat were concerned, it was necessary to unite all the anti-fascist forces; but this meant that positivist rationalism necessarily had to become a theoretical ally, and so the actual line of demarcation in the theoretical struggle ran between rationalism and irrationalism.

The irrational view of totality originally appeared in bourgeois thinking as the open subordination of the totality to the interests and standpoint of some select élite (as in Nietzsche). Fascist ideology introduced a change in this whereby, within the framework of a given national-racial "totality" (which was always considered organic), all kinds of particularity were seemingly negated and surmounted. (Perhaps the most characteristic example of this was Walter Darré's "Blood and Soil" programme.) Irrationalism of the openly cynical aristocratic kind never had any chance of attaining real mass influence. In order to become an ideology of the masses it would have been obliged to get rid of its very aristocratism and to appear as some kind of "socialism". It is true, of course, that these two types of irrationalism are to some extent different ways of fulfilling the same function: Wolfgang Harich has correctly pointed out that in the twentieth century exclusiveness has become an item for mass consumption. There is no doubt that nazi propaganda also exploited this. But fascism had to appear not as the kind of socialism that aims to protect the interests of one class against those of another, but as a movement radically opposed to all those social parties that have a particular appeal to one class or another, i.e. both "capitalism" and "marxism". Marcuse identified this specific feature of fascist ideology very clearly:

"The whole that it presents is not the unification achieved by the domination of *one* class within the framework of class society, but rather a unity that combines *all* classes, that is supposed to overcome the reality of class struggle and thus of classes themselves. . . . A classless society, in other words, is the goal, but a classless society on the basis of and within the framework of the existing class society."[11]

Fascism is not a negation of the basis and framework of the existing class society: therefore it is an expressly *bourgeois* ideology. But it opposes liberalism (and in this respect aristocratic irrationalism too) and so represents an illusory transcendence of particularity: therefore its *nature* is *petty* bourgeois. And precisely because it was a petty bourgeois theory, fascism could not have been the last throw of capitalism, its epilogue. Here, as further

19

on, I am using the term "petty bourgeois" in a quite undifferentiated way. Obviously, not *all* the social strata which supported fascism can be considered petty bourgeois in terms of their position in the organisation of production. But their consciousness is of a typically petty bourgeois nature, and this is one of the things I am attempting to prove in what follows.

Fascist ideology does not affect the bases and framework of the existing society because it does not negate the principle of private property. At the same time, it is able to influence broad sectors of the population who either feel their existence to be threatened within the system or have actually been driven out to the margins of society, i.e. they have no perspective or real basis of existence within the given system. These "outcasts" could not of course lose anything by a genuine revolution and socialist transformation. But they abstract from the fact that the revolution has lost its immediate reality; and precisely because they have been driven out and are now "déclassé" they do not possess the collective consciousness and solidarity which is the indispensable psychological basis of proletarian class consciousness, and which the proletariat has acquired in the course of its collective struggles over several decades. Therefore, they strive not for the radical transformation of the existing society but to recapture their "traditional" place within it.

It was not an accident that the mass base of the communists was formed by the "old" unemployed, those who had been factory workers for a long period of time (they were imbued with a consciousness of proletarian solidarity, and since their existence within the given system was not guaranteed, they strove to annihilate that system), whereas the "new" unemployed — who had been proletarianised out of a petty bourgeois, mostly peasant milieu and usually very soon became unemployed — joined the fascist camp. This stratum too (the lowest one, the "new" proletariat which had no class consciousness and the lumpenproletariat) readily accepted an ideology which in fact was only *adequate* for the traditional petty bourgeoisie, a different stratum altogether. Unlike the former, the traditional petty bourgeoisie had not yet lost the basis of its existence, but it felt threatened both by the increasing concentration of capital and by the organised economic struggle of the proletariat.* Fascism did not *deceive* the traditional petty bourgeoisie. It guaranteed their right to property. And furthermore, it offered them a perspective in which this guarantee was realisable: the assertion of the interests of the nation as a "totality" against other nations and races.

---

*The development of modern capitalism in the twentieth century and the intensification of the accumulation of capital did not lead to the annihilation of the middle classes, contrary to Marx's expectations. For example, in contemporary American society the middle classes are numerically very important and their proportion is even increasing. But the conditions of the traditional petty bourgeois existence — those of the independent small producer — have in fact been destroyed or are coming to an end. The later capitalism broke through in a country, the more elements of social compromise this process involved, and the more difficult and uneven was the transformation of its social structure. In this respect, too, the United States was in a very fortunate position. Since the bulk of its population had emigrated from Europe in the last century, its social structure adjusted easily to the requirements of economic transformation.

III The Explicit Doctrine of National Particularity

It is unnecessary to give a detailed account of the demagogically deceitful nature of the totalitarian principle in fascism. It is quite obvious that any one given nation or race, as opposed to other ones, is nothing but a particular formation. It is also obvious, even if it sounds paradoxical, that the representation of such a particular grouping's interests necessarily takes highly brutal and aggressive forms because it is *openly* particularistic, and is therefore built on an explicit negation of precisely those fundamental values which bourgeois development itself has produced. The point of departure for every type of bourgeois ideology is human individuality, and it is this that makes them *bourgeois* ideologies. They cannot turn into the ideology of "human emancipation" (Marx) while one of their preconditions is the egoistic man of "civil society" who strives to assert his own particular interests against all others, and while the other precondition is property:

"None of the so-called rights of man, therefore, go beyond egoistic man, beyond man as a member of civil society, that is, an individual withdrawn into himself, into the confines of his private interests and private caprice, and separated from the community. In the rights of man, he is far from being conceived as a species-being; on the contrary, species-life itself, society, appears as a framework external to the individuals, as a restriction of their original independence. The sole bond holding them together is natural necessity, need and private interest, the preservation of their property and their egoistic selves."[12]

However, because the bourgeois revolution destroyed the "naturally given limits" of earlier societies, it called the "citizen" into existence. It abolished the privileges of birth by making it possible in principle for everyone to move up to the top of the social ladder, and it transformed the individual — although in a purely "spiritual" form, the form of the political state — into the representative of the life of the species. "The perfected political state is man's *species life,* as *opposed* to his material life."[13] The *aim* of the bourgeois revolution is "human emancipation". But when this human emancipation "strives to realise itself under the form of political emancipation" (that is, when it constitutes man as a species-being divorced from his real, egoistic material existence in an isolated sphere, the political sphere) it creates a contradiction which can only be resolved by rendering the human species-life purely spiritual and by making it subordinate to man's real, material particularity:

"At times of special self-confidence, political life seeks to suppress its prerequisite, civil society and the elements composing this society, and to constitute itself as the real species-life of man devoid of contradictions. But it can achieve this only by coming into *violent* contradiction with its own conditions of life, only by declaring the revolution to be *permanent,* and therefore the political drama necessarily ends with the re-establishment of religion, private property, and all the elements of civil society, just as war ends with peace."[14]

The Jacobin petty bourgeoisie's attempt in 1793 to subordinate the "bourgeois" to the "citizen" was necessarily condemned because, as Marx says, it meant the abolition of life, the permanence of the guillotine, as long as the duality of bourgeois and citizen did not cease in real, material life. However, *"political* emancipation [i.e. the 'spiritual' postulation of man as a species-being] is, of course, a big step forward. True, it is not the final form of human emancipation in general, but it is the final form of human emancipation *within* the hitherto existing world order".[15] The movement of the fascist petty bourgeoisie of 1922 and the national socialist petty bourgeoisie of 1933 meant the *renunciation* of the specific form of human emancipation that was made ultimately possible by the conditions of the hitherto existing world order (i.e. capitalism). It meant total renunciation of the achievement of 1793, of the "spiritual" postulation of human emancipation. Goebbels's statement on the nazis' seizure of power was very characteristic: "By this we have obliterated the year 1789 from history!"

At the same time, it must be admitted that there are similarities between 1793 and fascism. The real social basis for the parallel is the fact that the petty bourgeoisie completely fails in its

23

attempt to solve, within the framework of bourgeois society, the fundamental contradiction between political equality in the realm of the spirit and practical-material inequality. But while the protagonists of 1793 strove to solve this contradiction by linking material equality (the equality of ownership) with political equality, fascism attempted to link practical-material equality (its highly characteristic permanent slogan was struggle against non-productive, parasitic, "Jewish" capital) with the complete denial of political equality, i.e. the denial of the only (spiritual) realisation of man's species-life that was possible within the capitalist system. Fascism thus renounced all the achievements through which bourgeois evolution had advanced on the way towards the realisation of human emancipation and of the human essence.

Since the bourgeois does not suffer from but on the contrary enjoys the results of this development, he is not in the least interested in seeing its contradictions dissolve. The class-conscious proletariat, on the other hand, as a class "being-for-itself", strives to solve the contradictions of capitalist society by putting an end to it. The characteristic trait of petty bourgeois ideologies and of the movements relying on them is their attempt to solve the fundamental contradictions of capitalist society *within* this society; it has been characteristic of them throughout the history of this society. But the petty bourgeoisie in the *nascent* capitalist society intended to put an end to the contradiction by means of the radical realisation of bourgeois principles, in the course of which they vainly called for the realisation of the human essence. The aims of the petty bourgeoisie in *established* capitalist society, on the other hand, represent only its own egoistic interests; it denies the species-essence of man and, in the fascist period, it openly denies even those values which the bourgeoisie itself has elaborated.

The nationalist and racist ideology of fascism is not an accidental element. This is demonstrated by the fact that the "uplifting" of the "nation", even at the expense of the very existence of other nations, is the only constant element in its very varied programmes, which in other respects are always subject to radical change. As we shall see later, the nazis insisted on this principle even after it had clearly become contrary to their power interests to do so. It was only the nationalist and racist ideology that enabled fascism to avoid conflict between, on the one hand, the particular interests of the masses who joined it and were represented by it, and on the other hand, the basic principles of the existing social system. Had such a conflict taken place, then first of all the bourgeoisie would not have allowed fascism to seize power, and secondly fascism would have been unable to secure any kind of mass support, since it would not have been acting as the specific opponent of (reformist) socialism. Again, the fact that German fascism considered itself to be "national socialism" was not some cheap deception, a propaganda slogan for the masses. It expressed the essence of the movement. It was socialism in the commonsense meaning of the word: it claimed to represent the particular interests of *all* the members of a given national community (in the sense of satisfying the material needs of all social strata on an ever-increasing scale), and it was at the same time necessarily nationalist, inasmuch as, not basing itself on the negation of its own existing society, it could only achieve its "socialistic" objectives at the expense of other nations. It was no coincidence that the so-called "national bolshevist" wing of German fascism, led by the Strasser brothers, gradually lost importance within the movement as the Hitler wing grew. Linking the nationalist idea with communistic aims *taken seriously*, i.e. directed at the abolition of private property, would not have provided the movement with any basis. The ruling classes would not accept it and were forced to oppose it very strongly. Understandably this wing was not liked, either, by the strata who formed the actual mass base of nazism, whose aims were to secure their little bits of property and to maintain their middle-class position. On the other hand the proletariat, if it has a genuinely revolutionary consciousness and not a petty-bourgeois "rebellious" one, is the class least receptive to nationalist ideas. And those strata within the working class who are most receptive to nationalist ideas are generally not revolutionary.

Not only the nationalist idea but also its *aggressive* manifestations followed from the petty bourgeoisie's aims. The defence of national sovereignty on its own would not have made the realisation of "socialist" aims at all possible. Fascism did not have to defend the equality of its own people against other peoples (although the "injustice" of the Versailles treaty terms as they affected Germany were very advantageous to nazism). But it had to satisfy the particular interests of its own people expressly at the expense of other nations. It was this which led on to the denial of the values defended (even if only in the realm of the "spirit") by the bourgeoisie, and above all to the negation of the idea of equality. Until the appearance of fascism, "normal" capitalist society, even when it produced the most conspicuous inequalities, still maintained the idea of equality and defended this idea in the form of equality before the law. Of course, not even this kind of equality has actually come about, but nevertheless its maintenance in principle has meant a real advance on all preceding social formations.

Fascism is a bourgeois ideology which revokes the bourgeois idea of equality, and regresses even further, to a denial of the idea of equality proclaimed by christianity. The idea of a superior race (which is simply the "scientific" formulation for the rights of one particular nation in opposition to others) is the means of eliminating class conflict within the given nation, and is an open declaration of the inequality of the human species. (The idea itself, of course, was not born with the fascist movement; but its ideological elaboration belongs to the immediate prehistory of fascism.)

Fascism, or the fascist state, is not the first bourgeois form of power to conduct wars of conquest at the expense of other nations. But it is the first bourgeois form of power to openly proclaim aggressive expansionist aims against peoples that live at an essentially identical economic and cultural level and in an identical social system. The most barbaric colonial wars of the bourgeois states have been fought first of all under the guise of "civilising" the underdeveloped countries, and secondly against peoples whose actual economic and cultural underdevelopment was undeniable, whose "inferiority" was "verified" by "facts", and not by some irrational mysticism about race.

Therefore the brutality and unscrupulous cruelty of fascism are not the result of the "brutalisation" of the haute bourgeoisie at the highest level of power. The barbarity of fascism comes from those strata which feel their existence threatened *in* capitalist society — and not by its possible overthrow — or by those driven to the peripheries of this society, whose movement and ideology strive at whatever cost to get rid of the contradictions of the society within the given system. In this respect, at least, fascism is capitalist society's "last word", the most brutal possible unmasking of its internal contradictions. Its brutality is due to the fact that it removes all the "inhibitions" of the strata struggling for life, for *bare* existence — inhibitions which had been created by the ideal of equality (even if only in the "spiritual" sense), itself the result of bourgeois development.

IV The Fear of Freedom and the Negation of Democracy

So far I have been discussing the renunciation of the bourgeois ideal of equality and its effects. But fascism is also the negation of that other fundamental bourgeois ideal, the ideal of liberty. The formula is the same. In fascism the negation of the ideal of liberty appears as the negation of bourgeois democracy. Fascists identify bourgeois democracy with the right of various different groups to assert their own particular interests at the expense of the totality. It should be added that this is justified. The essence of bourgeois democracy consists (a) in the fact that the various particular groups may dispose freely of the representation of their interests, and (b) in the belief that the struggle of these particular groups and the conflict of the particular interests will produce a social system which best suits the interests of the totality. Since as a result the particular interests of important strata are completely ignored (despite the proposed harmony), fascism proposes the negation of bourgeois democracy. Here again it is the interests of the petty bourgeoisie that are the determining ones.

Because of the intensive and extensive growth of capitalist concentration, which had the result of strengthening the working class in numbers and in organisation, the living standards and even the existence of the petty bourgeoisie and of the traditional middle strata began to be threatened in bourgeois democracy. In Italy and Germany at least, the trends of development certainly pointed in this direction. A considerable number of those who belonged to these strata had ceased to be petty bourgeois, in the social sense of the word; it was only their petty bourgeois consciousness that they preserved. (The déclassé elements were increasing considerably as a result of the world war; the great majority of fascist leaders came from their ranks.) Bourgeois democracy seemed to suit the interests of two classes only: the power élite composed of members of the haute bourgeoisie, and the working class inasmuch as it became integrated into the system by having its economic "particular" needs partially satisfied. But bourgeois democracy could not satisfy the middle classes. They had no form of organisation like the working class's trade unions with which to fight for and achieve the satisfaction of their interests, even if it had been economically possible to maintain independent small-scale enterprises. The workers, through their trade-union struggles, were able to strive for and actually achieve an acceptable standard of living in both countries, within the circumstances. The petty bourgeoisie, however, gradually went bankrupt. As a result, the latter turned with a bitter vehemence against the working class: the have-nots were living better than the petty bourgeoisie themselves, "at their expense". Gramsci wrote that fascism "made use of and organised the irresponsibility of the petty bourgeoisie, as well as its cowardice and stupidity, of that petty bourgeoisie which hated the working class because the latter had succeeded through the power of its organisations in mitigating the blows of the capitalist crisis".[16]

Both in Italy and in Germany, the petty bourgeoisie was the losing party in the bourgeois democracy; it possessed no forms of organisation which might enable it to realise the opportunities offered by parliamentary democracy. So the petty bourgeoisie turned against democracy; but they obviously remained based on bourgeois society, retaining the principles of private property. And this necessarily implied the negation of any kind of democracy or liberty.

I have already said that the negation of the bourgeois ideal of liberty presents us with the same formula as does the negation of the ideal of equality. The negation of bourgeois democracy is the negation of the bourgeoisie's realisation of its own ideal of liberty; although the fascist critique of the contradictions of bourgeois democracy is completely justified, it leads to the *explicit* negation of the bourgeois ideal of liberty itself. Fascism is the bourgeois ideology which actually revokes the idea of liberty, rather than simply restricting it in practice whenever its interests demand such a restriction.

In the bourgeois conception of liberty, freedom is tied exclusively to the individual, in the sense of the formula: "I do what I like as far as I have the power to do so." Consequently, the limits of one individual's freedom are set by the freedom of others. The restriction of the freedom of others derives from the "citizen" principle of freedom itself. But in the material world of the bourgeoisie, the spiritual, "citizen" ideal of freedom means the freedom to restrict others.

By revoking this ideal of liberty, fascist ideology is simply announcing the truth of the given society and uncovering the falsity of the ideal of liberty in the bourgeois world. It elevates the actual practice of this society to the status of a *principle*. But it also means a regression from the achievements of the bourgeois world which has been advancing (though by way of contradictions) along the path of the realisation of the human species-essence. In bourgeois society, freedom exists only as a postulate; but to negate this postulate means to renounce a world where human liberty may be realised.

V The Fascistoid Character

It seems to be completely rational for fascism to revoke the ideal of equality: that is to say, it can be deduced from the particular interests of the fascist movement's participants. The renunciation of the ideal of freedom, on the other hand, i.e. the negation not only of the freedom of other nations and "races" but also of one's own personal freedom, is problematical, and a purely sociological explanation would seem to be insufficient.

But the "rationality" of revoking the ideal of equality is also only an *apparent* rationality. It can be accounted for by the particular interests of the fascist movement's participants; but there are "socio-psychological" aspects behind this, just as there are behind the renunciation of the ideal of freedom. The only difference is that when the ideal of equality is revoked, the socio-psychological factor is so obvious that it gets overlooked. The acceptability of a specific action or ideology simply presupposes that the psychological personality type who acts or accepts the ideology is basing himself on his own particular interests or those of his group: in bourgeois society, the acceptance of this action or ideology is *apparently rational,* since the fundamental condition for the normal functioning of this society is the "particular" personality, whose character-structure is based on the drive "to have" and whose sole objective is held to be the satisfaction of his own material interests and those of the group.

Revoking the ideal of freedom, on the other hand, points to something different. The complete identification of the individual with his group, the absolute surrender of his own personality to the interests of the "community" and to power, the unconditional obedience to the "Führer" who takes self-sacrifice for granted: all these things, in contrast, presuppose a character type which is *apparently in contradiction with* the normal individuals of bourgeois society, and therefore seems to be entirely "irrational". It is this aspect of the fascist movement, this specific characteristic of its participants, that has induced many investigators of fascism to look at its "socio-psychological" basis.

31

It goes without saying that the only investigations which are important to a marxist analysis of fascism are those which do not try to explain fascism in its totality with the *help* of social psychology, but try to analyse the "socio-psychological" *basis* of fascism, i.e. to describe and explain the type of personality whose existence was made possible by the emergence of a fascist mass movement and who in turn enabled fascism to take power. Attempts to "deduce" fascism itself from the "authoritarian" character of the individuals or nations concerned are theoretically quite unacceptable. There are some books in the field of social psychology which I find interesting from the theoretical aspect because of the way they pose the question: I am thinking of Wilhelm Reich's *The Mass Psychology of Fascism*, Erich Fromm's *Fear of Freedom*, and *The Authoritarian Personality* by Theodor Adorno and others. Since it is not my purpose to study the various theories of fascism, I shall not analyse these works but simply indicate that, in several respects, I disagree with them.

The implicit or explicit conclusion reached by every analyst of the "social psychology" of fascism who calls himself a marxist can be summed up as follows. The character of the individuals who form the mass base of the fascist movement is not a specifically fascistoid one which never existed before and only arose in the fascist period. It is a personality structure which is widespread in the society, and manifests characteristics which are typical of its middle layers everywhere and in every period. It may be true, of course, that owing to certain historical circumstances the character traits necessary for the formation of fascism as a mass movement are more present in the make-up of the average petty bourgeois in some countries than they are elsewhere. But if we believe character as a whole to be a social and not a biological complex, then it would in fact be incomprehensible if social structures which are basically identical were to produce decisively different character-types. I do not want to deny that forms of bourgeois society vary in time and place, and bring about important personality differences in the typical individuals of the various classes and layers. But these differences cannot explain the appearance of fascism and its growth into a mass movement. Had the solution of economic and social problems demanded it, there would have been layers in *any* modern society whose members' typical personality would have suited them for participation in

32

fascist movements, and on a mass scale. Fascism cannot be deduced from the "national character": the demonstrable difference between the "national character" of the citizens of Germany and Italy makes that much obvious. What can be deduced from it, however, are certain characteristic features of the fascist movement and fascist power, although I shall not be using this particular factor when I come to explain the different fates and contradictory features of the two fascist powers.

Of the typical character traits of the members of the middle layers in bourgeois society, which ones constitute the psychological basis for the individual's participation in the fascist movement? I wish to emphasise once again that in this respect, the status of the middle layers is not solely nor even fundamentally determined by the position they occupy in the organisation of production. Since character traits are formed in childhood, the primary determining medium for the formation of petty bourgeois character traits is the everyday life of the family, for this is what constitutes the child's basic environment. If the family structure is typically petty bourgeois, then the social status of the person or persons who provide for the family is not decisive in the formation of the growing child's character. The fundamental merit of Wilhelm Reich's work is that he recognised this and brought it out, although I disagree with his freudian account of the "mechanism" of character formation.

The typical character traits are as follows:

1) There is a focusing on particularity: an uncritical relationship to one's own self. One's needs, desires and ideas are simply something given. (On the question of particularity and the differentiation between the "particular personality" and the "Individual", I have relied considerably here and in what follows on Agnes Heller's book *Everyday Life* [translation of Hungarian title].[17])

2) The particular personality's uncritical relationship to his own self is always accompanied by an uncritical relationship to the particular group which is accidentally given. The group to which he is affiliated represents, for him, the human species: he identifies himself completely with the non-chosen group to which he belongs (his family, his nation etc.), and accepts their scale of values as "natural", as the only unconditionally valid ones. His relationship to this "natural" group is carried over into his rela-

33

tionship to a "freely chosen" community: when the particular personality "freely" joins an accidentally given community, this act does not differ very much from the chance event of being born into a group. A genuinely chosen (i.e. non-accidental) group affiliation presupposes not only that we assess the pros and cons before we join it, but also that *after* we have joined the group we continue to maintain a conscious relationship to the scale of values and the attitudes of that group. As a result of this, various kinds of conflict may arise which can sometimes lead to a decisive stand being made against the group originally chosen, even if at the outset the identification was complete. But the type we are examining uncritically accepts all the changes of value and attitude which his seemingly chosen group may undergo, and thus exposes the uncritical nature of the affiliation itself. Of course, even this type of personality may eventually break with his "natural" or "quasi-chosen" group. But the turnabout is always absolute: complete identification lapses into complete rejection.

3) The consequence of this attitude is that the "particular personality" rigidly divides society into in-groups and out-groups. He regards society as a network of narrower and wider groups focused on himself. He identifies himself with the in-group at every level, and whenever the realisation of the in-group's aims is hindered for some reason, he throws the responsibility on the out-group or out-groups and vehemently turns against them. One example of a widening network of in-groups is family — kinfolk — village community — nation — race. If family affairs are in bad shape, the kinfolk are responsible because they have done the family out of its inheritance; for the misery of one's own nation it is the surrounding countries which are to blame, because they have stolen its *Lebensraum*; for the problems of the Aryan race it is the inferior races who are to blame, etc.

4) There is a conservative orientation towards the past. The particular personality idealises the "original" life-situation of the years when he was growing up (basically the family and the nation), and accepts it unreservedly. If his demands are unsatisfied, he rebels against those who in his opinion are responsible for his misery or that of his particular group (but only if *his own* demands remain unsatisfied, since otherwise he does not notice the drop in his in-group's material position and status). He always looks for — and finds — the scapegoat in some group of persons

34

(this is where the root of anti-semitism lies). He may also rebel against an existing structure if it favours the out-groups, his scapegoats; but in this case he fights for the restoration of the "original" structure. However radical his revolt, it is always directed back towards the past. He cannot become a revolutionary, for this would demand a critical attitude towards the "original" situation of the in-group. I put the word "original" in quotation marks because the particular personality's ideas about the "golden age" of his family, nation or race are usually a long way from being the truth about what actually used to exist. But this golden age *must* have existed, because his attention is concentrated on the situation of his own family (nation, race, etc.) and this, in principle, must have been the most perfect one possible.

5) Finally, there is his authoritarian attitude. He rebels only when he senses that the governing power is weak and ripe for overthrow, i.e. when it is no longer a real power. On the other hand he defies the real, strong power, or at least the one that appears strong to him; he regards it as a transcendent power — its commands are not just fulfilled, they *must* be fulfilled. He shifts all responsibility for his own life and actions on to the absolute authority. But towards the weak, on the other hand, he considers himself an unconditional authority, and in this relationship it is he himself who is the transcendent power — his every demand is an order that must be unconditionally fulfilled.

It goes without saying that the above-mentioned characteristics are in fact typical of the average "petty bourgeois" in bourgeois society, and are not characteristic of fascists alone. Nevertheless, analysis reveals that fascism actually exploited them skilfully: to be more precise, fascist ideology was really based on an idealised model of just these characteristics. (The fascist leaders themselves were also people of this type. They did not have to "invent" an ideology to dazzle and conquer the masses with. Far from it: their ideology actually corresponded to their own character.[18])

All these character traits are indispensable for the functioning not only of fascism but also of manipulated pseudo-democracy (the society of "organised irresponsibility"). There is one important aspect which we have not mentioned so far, however, and which seems to be characteristic only of the fascist type. When a conflict situation arises, the tiered levels of in-groups seem, for the fascist type, to have a hierarchy of value, and he does not identify himself unconditionally with those in-groups which are of smaller extent. The logical consequence of the in-group/out-group structure, which is built on particularity, should be that the individual unconditionally puts his own interests before those of the in-group, and the interests of the smaller and more immediate in-group before those of the bigger and more widely extended one: that is to say, he defends his own interests against his family, those of his family against those of the nation, etc. But this is not characteristic of fascists, at least not in the majority of cases. The "convinced" fascist is self-sacrificing. Also, he can easily be turned against his family for the sake of the "nation": in fascist countries, members of the same family frequently and characteristically denounce each other, which is a very convenient way for those in power to control people who try to keep their heads down.

In my opinion, however, it is the circumstances, not character traits, that determine whether or not this aspect of the in-group/out-group structure asserts itself in a conflict situation. The authoritarian character identifies himself with all his in-groups in all circumstances; and for the fascist, too, there is a moral obligation to be an outstanding father, mother or child, and to defend the interests of his or her family against other families. But even when the iron-fisted power attacks his immediate in-group, even when it attacks himself, he does not turn against it, precisely because the hierarchy of in-groups is *not a hierarchy of values*. And this is not only a feature of fascism. We only have to look at the enthusiastic self-sacrifice made by the citizens of the democratic countries during the first world war. Because the authoritarian character does not have his own hierarchy of values, he always identifies himself automatically with the hierarchy of values of his accidentally given group. If these groups come into conflict with each other, he sides with the hierarchy of values of the stronger and more powerful group: he "chooses" the latter. But why does he go so far with this identification as to sacrifice himself as well, especially if it is true that his entire world is ordered around his own particularity? The paradox is only an apparent one. Because he has no hierarchy of values, because he has no values in whose name he might oppose the hierarchy of values of his "community" (i.e. his accidentally given particular group) and because he is linked to the human species *only* through his particular groups, then the repudiation of all his in-groups would, for him, mean the surrender of his very existence as a human being and excommunication from the human community, in other words his annihilation. This is why he obeys the commands of the most powerful in-group even when it means his own self-annihilation. If the "strongest" power — which is always almighty for him — demands his life, then his life is lost, for one cannot oppose the strongest power. No basis for such a possibility exists.

I have not discussed the fascistoid character trait which is often discussed first: brutality. I have not done so for two reasons. First of all, if we regard Italian fascism and German national socialism as historically identical formations, then we cannot consider nazi brutality (which certainly surpassed the "average" historical level of brutality) as a necessary trait of fascism. The kind of brutality carried out by the Italian fascist movement and dictatorship is certainly not unique even in modern history, let alone in the periods before the ideal of humanity arose. It is impossible to avoid attributing a certain role in this respect to the national character. Nazi brutality is assured of a conspicuous place in the history of human atrocities precisely because of its organised and "large-scale" nature. The connection between this phenomenon (which was, of course, historically formed) and the German (primarily the Prussian) national character has been pointed out by so many writers that it is not necessary to analyse it in detail, and I will simply refer the reader in particular to Georg Lukács's essay "Uber Preussentum".[19]

My second reason for not going thoroughly into the question of brutality is that I do not believe it to be a permanent trait. The authoritarian character always asserts the interests of his in-group against the weak in the most brutal way afforded him by the framework of possibilities. Brutality cannot become a permanent character trait: it has to be *socially admissible*. A German or Italian fascist may have been the most tender-hearted father or husband possible; he was only unconditionally brutal towards his actual or presumed enemy. And even in those bourgeois societies where the political structure is as democratic as it could be, the average petty bourgeois is usually brutal in those relationships where the laws and norms of the society permit it.

I shall now deal briefly with the question of why the "authoritarian" personality type under examination is primarily characteristic of the middle layers of bourgeois society, and with the "mechanism" of its rise.

It needs to be said that the particularity-oriented structure of the personality which we have examined, and the direct consequences of this orientation (a more or less uncritical relation to the particular group, the consciousness's division of society into in-group and out-group), are characteristic of every average person in bourgeois society, and are in fact generally characteristic of "pre-historic" man and his alienated social formations. In every society that has so far existed, individuality in the proper sense of the term has been an exception. While conservatism and authoritarian behaviour are typical "petty bourgeois" traits, let it be said at once that they are to be observed among other layers as well.

As Marx put it, bourgeois society completed the severing of the individual from the community's umbilical cord. The individual became free: his origin no longer necessarily determined either his social rank, or his position in the social division of labour, or his way of life. Even in periods of bourgeois society where social mobility is least (and even here the mobility is greater than it had been in preceding societies), it is possible, at least in principle, for anyone to climb to the top or sink to the bottom. The individual has, in fact, become master of his own fate, even if in the overwhelming majority of cases he needs extraordinary abilities (not necessarily abilities with a positive value content) or extraordinary good luck in order to rise from the layer he was born into. The individual has become free, he has been freed from the "naturally given" [naturwüchsig] restrictions of society. But only in exceptional cases can he realise this freedom.

The danger of downward mobility, on the other hand, is a constant threat to the individual who comes from the ruling classes of society. But downward mobility is just as exceptional as upward mobility. If a person possesses the material means indispensable for success by virtue of his birth, if being born into the ruling class means that he can acquire sufficient knowledge and education with relatively little effort, and if he has been accustomed to power since childhood, then he really must be "endowed" with capacities well below the average if he is not to "succeed in life". For the ruling class, freedom is a real possibility: it is the real possibility, as we have said, of restricting the

38

freedom of others. Consequently, the members of the ruling class are not necessarily conservative. Apart from a radical transformation of the total social structure, i.e. a genuine social revolution, there is no change which they cannot exploit for their own benefit. They can take risks: the failure of an enterprise will mean annihilation or misery for them only in very exceptional cases. "Receptivity towards what is new" is much more characteristic of the average member of the haute bourgeoisie than conservatism is: they have, after all, an "enterprising" spirit.

Authoritarian behaviour is not necessarily a ruling-class characteristic either. They acknowledge no authority over themselves, and because they have confidence in their own power and abilities they have no need of an authority to rely on or to shift responsibility to. Nor, since their social status is beyond question, do they have any need to be constantly proving their strength and power to the weaker people below them.

It does not take a lot of argument to prove that the proletarians, who are at the lowest level of society and who are *not* petty bourgeois in their conduct, have no need to be either conservative or authoritarian. What have they to lose? What higher power can create any further deterioration in their position or give them cause for hope? The proletarian learns very quickly that proletarian solidarity against the capitalist is a more effective weapon than adjusting to him.

Conservatism and authoritarian behaviour are therefore "normal" and average only for the middle classes. They are conservative because they cannot use the freedom which they are granted in principle; they cling to the given because this has some solid meaning for them, and they know very well that their chances of ascending are extremely slight. Their behaviour is authoritarian because they feel themselves to be entirely at the mercy of others (more so than the proletariat, which has nothing to lose), and consequently they behave like representatives of authority towards those below them who are weaker — not only to compensate for their defencelessness, but also because they sense that the slightest weakness or concession on their part might lead to their downfall. In addition to this, the view of society based on an in-group/out-group division, and the behaviour which corresponds to this view, are much more *rigid* amongst the middle classes than in any other layers of society. It is the middle classes who, because of their position in the social structure of production, are not only opposed to the layers below and above them but are also constantly coming into conflict with members of their own layer. The traditional petty bourgeois — the artisan, the smallholder, the retailer — is more affected by competition; the position of the "new" middle class is similar, though the conditions are different. "White-collar workers" also necessarily compete against each other.

The "fear of freedom" which is expressed in conservatism and authoritarian behaviour is by no means an irrational, incomprehensible trait of the "average person" in bourgeois society. I am completely in agreement with Erich Fromm's statement that "if the economic, social and political conditions on which the whole process of human individuation depends do not offer a basis for the realisation of individuality . . . while at the same time people have lost those ties which gave them security, this lag makes freedom an unbearable burden".[20] I also agree that in the twentieth century, with the development of monopoly capitalism, this feeling has necessarily intensified:

> "The individual's feeling of powerlessness and aloneness has increased, his 'freedom' from all traditional bonds has become more pronounced, his possibilities for individual economic achievement have narrowed down. He feels threatened by gigantic forces and the situation resembles in many ways that of the fifteenth and sixteenth centuries."[21]

The "workshop" for the formation of the authoritarian personality type is the petty bourgeois family. The psychic structure of the personality is built on particular features given to him when he "enters the world", and is already shaped and fixed in early childhood; the given family structure ensures that it corresponds basically to the objective demands which guarantee the functioning of the given social order. (This is why personality structures which are "typical" of one layer also reappear in other layers.) I do not propose to discuss here the way in which the family structure determines the psychic character, or the mechanisms which form the personality structure; for this discussion, the reader is referred to the essay "Family Structure and Communism", written jointly by Agnes Heller and myself (see *The Humanisation of Socialism: Writings of the Budapest School*, London, 1976).

40

Fascism obviously relies to a large extent on that view of society which is based on the in-group/out-group structure and which is widespread among the middle layers; it relies on their rigidity and their authoritarian behaviour. The connection between fascism and the petty bourgeois layers' conservatism needs little explanation either. I have already pointed out that this conservatism does not mean permanent acquiescence in the situation as temporarily given: far from it. But what it does mean is that when the members of the middle layer mobilise against a situation, they do not try to transform the social conditions but to call to account the people "responsible" for that situation, and if need be to annihilate them. This also explains why the masses allow fascism to deceive them, in a certain sense. I do not mean that the fascist leaders consciously misled the masses with promises which they themselves thought to be unrealisable, for they mostly deceived themselves too. They deceived themselves and others because in many cases the demands which they promised to fulfil were actually incompatible with each other. But essentially their promises pointed towards transformations in the sphere of politics (which in bourgeois society is, generally speaking, more or less irrelevant for the masses), by which all layers would be guaranteed the ability to carry on their accustomed way of life, accompanied by enhanced satisfaction of their material needs. The fascist leaders were going to raise the whole "nation", and would not allow the egoistical interests of any one class to be asserted against another ("socialism"). What gave fascism its mass effect was precisely the fact that it supplied the conservative rebellion with an ideology and, equally important, with an organisational framework.

VI The "Combat Troop" as an Organisational Form

These ideas, with their petty bourgeois content, needed a framework, they needed an adequate organisational form if they were to be fulfilled. What were the organisational forms which fascism, as a petty bourgeois movement, was able to develop to the point where it could replace the liberal bourgeois state power with its own dictatorship?

My analysis so far has demonstrated clearly that the ideology of the fascist movement was expressly a "petty bourgeois" one, whose aggressiveness presented an intensified version of the worldview and psychology of the average member of the middle classes. Its intensified character can be explained by the suddenly heightened feeling of insecurity, and by the fact that a considerable part of the masses had already been driven out of production and become déclassé. The evidence available shows that the social composition of both Italian fascism from the beginning of the twenties and the German national socialist movement at the end of the twenties and beginning of the thirties, consisted of "petty bourgeois" elements, mainly members of the urban middle classes and déclassé petty bourgeoisie. But the peasants who formed the middle classes in the villages also played an important role in the nazi seizure of power (they were the fascists' voters).

The fascist movement created a form of organisation which, in a certain sense, is unique in history. The decisive element in the movement was certainly not the fascist or national socialist party: in comparison with the armed organisations such as the stormtroopers, the party as such played an almost insignificant role. The character of the movement itself was determined not by the party but by the armed forms of organisation. The party's job was to enable the movement to make a complementary use of parliamentary tactics in the struggle for power, and thereby to obtain for itself an important conservative base as well.

Various authors have already pointed out that one of the basic characteristics of fascism was its "stormtrooper tactics" (the

42

Stosstrup-Taktik), and that the real fascist movement was born at the moment the stormtroopers were established. Perhaps no one saw the importance of this as clearly as Gramsci, who in the columns of *Ordine Nuovo* kept a close watch on the formation of the fascist movement in 1919. He did not merely recognise the elements of which these stormtroopers were made up, their function, and the use made of them by the ruling bourgeoisie for its own purposes; he also realised that *for the first time in history, the petty bourgeoisie had found its own adequate organisational form.*

As early as the summer of 1919, he clearly saw what the terrible consequences would be if the revolutionary movement were to find itself unable to take hold of the activity of the masses, which had been aroused by the war-induced crisis and by the collective experiences of the petty bourgeois layers and the peasantry during the war, and guide it into its own channels, turning it against the existing capitalist régime:

"The spiritual results of the war period, the communistic and collective experiences accumulated in the dirty and bloody trenches in the course of four years of bloody sacrifice, may well be wasted if all the individuals cannot be united in the organisations of the new collective life, consolidating these results, developing and integrating the practical experiences and directing itself consciously towards a concrete historical aim. Thus organised, the peasants will become the elements of order and progress; but if they are left to themselves without being able to follow a systematic and disciplined activity, then they will become an uncontrollable mass, a chaos of desperate passions which will produce the most terrible barbarity and unheard-of suffering."[22]

In 1921, discussing the experience of the Italian fascist movement and the Spanish events, Gramsci could already clearly see the breeding ground and aims of this petty-bourgeois mass movement: "There exists a layer of the population in every country — the petty and middle bourgeoisie — which believes that it can solve the gigantic problems with machine-guns and pistols, and this layer is the breeding ground of fascism and supplies its cadres".[23] Gramsci wanted to know why this petty bourgeois mass movement had developed. He was probably the first person to give a concrete answer to this question, discovering the reasons in the

43

economic development of the country and not contenting himself with simple accounts of the crisis situation, the post-war disintegration, or the decomposition of previously intact social layers as a result of the ravages of war. Undoubtedly these latter aspects played an important part in forming a layer which had completely lost its social bearings and strived for a change at all costs. In the beginning, therefore, it joined the developing revolutionary movements; but after experiencing the failure of the revolution it went over to fascism, hoping that the latter would solve the crisis. These déclassé elements from the war period, however, were joined by petty bourgeois layers whom the development of capitalism had forced to give up their original way of life, and who were consciously and *from the beginning* opposed to the armed organisations of the working class. These layers rejected a real revolutionary movement in any case; they were not willing to display solidarity with any kind of proletarian activity, for they were not disillusioned revolutionaries but petty bourgeois rebels:

> "Wealth flows from the petty and middle bourgeoisie to the haute bourgeoisie, *without any further development of the apparatus of production* [my italics — M.V.]."[24]

Gramsci clearly saw, therefore, that fascism was not simply and directly caused by the turmoil of the war period and by a crisis which had failed to grow into a revolution, but that it was the product of unfolding economic processes. He was the first to realise that the mass base of fascism was created by the structural change in capitalism. The reformist socialists were inclined to explain fascism as the result of war psychosis, and consequently did not attach a great deal of importance to it. They were inclined to think that once the functioning of the economy had been restored to normal, fascism would vanish as quickly as it had appeared. The fascist movement was in fact an organised mass movement of the petty bourgeoisie, who felt their accustomed way of life to be threatened. But it was only possible to realise this by going beyond the mere phenomenological description of the situation in the particular countries, and seeing the phenomenon not only as the result of events which had already taken place but also from the standpoint of developing trends. Gramsci correctly understood the nature of the developing concentration of capital, and realised that in Italy the petty bourgeoisie's situation had become increasingly hopeless and that it had been obliged to create

44

its own organisation. And he saw the specific feature of fascism as being precisely the fact that this was occurring for the first time ever in the course of history:

"The characteristic trait of fascism consists in its success in having created a mass movement for the petty bourgeoisie. The originality of fascism lies in the fact that it has found an adequate organisational form for a social class which has always been unable to develop a unified structure and a unified ideology. This organisational form is the camp. The militia is the springboard of the *Partito Nazionale Fascista*. The militia cannot be dissolved without thereby dissolving the whole of the party itself."[25]

No other kind of organisational form could have been adequate for the petty bourgeoise. It could not have created the kind of organisations with which the working class defended their economic interests. Trade-union struggles and working-class strikes are successful because the proletariat is an indispensable element in the organisation of capitalist production. When it resists, it paralyses production. But the hopeless position of the petty bourgeoisie originated precisely from the fact that it had been at least partially driven out of the organisation of modern production. (There are, of course, the middle classes in the neo-capitalist structure too and they play a very important role, but this is a different question. There are various important ways in which the way of life of the "new" middle classes is different from that of the "old"; the transition from the old structure to the new has been necessarily accompanied by the dissolution of the old forms, quite apart from the fact that the new middle class is not necessarily formed out of members of the old one.)

It was equally hopeless for the petty bourgeoisie to try and form a party in the traditional bourgeois sense: for a party to succeed, or at least to have some hope of success in the parliamentary struggle, it must have some positive programme, and the petty bourgeoisie cannot have such a programme because it is afraid of any kind of change and its objectives are limited to reinforcing its shaken position. Its programme is a mere negation: the negation of the contradictions of capitalism, but within the framework of capitalism.

On the other hand, the "camp" and the armed combat troops corresponded to both the ideology of the movement and the character of its participants. I have already said that the social model which is built on the in-group/out-group structure necessarily considers the out-groups to be hostile, threatening powers. As soon as the petty bourgeois finds his lot becoming unbearable and sees the ground beginning to slip from under his feet, he immediately starts looking for the hostile group which can be blamed for his predicament. Since the crisis was permanent (in those countries which were en route to fascism), the petty bourgeois, realising that he was on a downward curve, felt that his "nation" was being threatened by other nations. It is typical of fascists that they considered all layers, classes, parties and individuals who were hostile to the fascist movement to be representatives and agents of a foreign power or race.

The combat organisation is obviously the most adequate organisational form with which to meet a danger which threatens "physically". And at the same time, the individuals joining these organisations immediately felt that there was an authority to rely on and that they did not have to shoulder personal responsibility any more. This organisational form naturally gave them a feeling of security and stability and enabled them to turn, freed from all personal responsibility, against all those who they felt threatened their existence.

This organisational form, which corresponds to the ideology and psyche of the petty bourgeois, can of course exist only temporarily, and only in crisis situations. But at other times the petty bourgeois does not actually need any kind of organisation. In periods when society is functioning wholly or relatively free from frictions, the petty bourgeois does not want to ally himself with anyone at all: in such periods he and his family "compete" along with the rest of society.

As an organisational form, the stormtroopers found the threatened sections of society, and above all the working class, entirely unprepared and helpless; they really did strengthen the petty bourgeois movement, enabling it to destroy working-class organisations and to acquire sufficient power in the course of this struggle to subsequently seize the state apparatus. The fact that once the petty bourgeois movement has seized power it carries out the bourgeoisie's programme (or at least that of part of the bourgeoisie), rather than its own, simply follows from the fact that it has no programme except the seizure of power. To put it more pre-

cisely, when the petty bourgeois movement carries out a programme of aggressive expansion it is thereby representing at
least as much the interests of the haute bourgeoisie as its own.
However, this has to do with the nature of fascist power rather
than that of the movement.

The petty bourgeois nature of the fascist *movement*, and the
fact that this particular form of the movement represented the
adequate organisational form of the petty bourgeoisie, remain —
even if, once fascism had seized power, it did not carry out the
"particular objectives" of the petty bourgeoisie. Nor was the petty
bourgeois nature of the movement altered by the fact that even
while it was emerging, it represented particular petty bourgeois
interests in such a way that it was also quite definitely contribut-
ing to the power of the bourgeoisie. This is why I cannot agree
with the conclusions drawn by Angelo Tasca, whose *The Rise
of Italian Fascism*[26] has in other respects added some important
elements to the marxist theory of fascism. Tasca denied the petty
bourgeois nature of fascism on the grounds that, by fighting
against the working class, it was siding with the bourgeoisie.[27] It
cannot be denied that fascism sided with the bourgeoisie. But I
am convinced that a social investigation which confines itself to
asking whose interests a particular movement serves in the final
analysis will always prove to be insufficient. If we pose the
question like this we cannot carry out a concrete analysis of any
kind of social situation from the viewpoint of the proletariat. The
problem is not whether fascism serves the bourgeoisie's interests
in the final analysis, since in the final analysis this statement would
prove to be true of any movement that does not want to overthrow the existing bourgeois system in a revolutionary way. The
problem is *how* does it serve those interests? In the case of
fascism, the "how" is accounted for precisely by its petty bourgeois character. According to Tasca:

> "Fascism is pure reaction, but a reaction which applies the
> only effective mass methods in the postwar situation. . . .
> However, the specific 'originality' of fascism consists far less
> in its mass 'tactics' or demagogic programme than in the
> determining and, from a certain point of view, autonomous
> function which these tactics acquire at the expense of the
> programme. . . . Fascism conducts its war for posts rather
> than for principles. . . . This explains the role which organisa-

47

tion, and above all armed organisation, plays in fascism."[28] He then goes on to enumerate some very important elements in the make-up of fascism, but he does not account for their roots. It is beyond doubt a fact that in fascism, tactics take priority over the programme; this is a simple consequence of the movement's lack of an actual programme. It is also true that fascism's only real aim is to seize power, and that the only thing it can do with this power is defend it constantly. I have also already pointed out that if tactics take priority, then armed organisation is the only adequate organisational form. But the source of all these interrelated aspects lies in the petty bourgeois nature of fascism and they all confirm it. If this were not so, then the only way to explain their origin would be to state that the bourgeoisie invented this movement for its own purposes. From this it would follow, however, that fascism in power was actually the direct power of the bourgeoisie itself; and Tasca even denies this himself, in fact, when he says that fascism in power is the rule of a *new class* with which the bourgeoisie has entered into a compromise.[29]

Tasca's denial of the petty bourgeois nature of the fascist movement leads to a mistaken estimate of the strength of fascist power, just as the official Comintern standpoint did.

CRISIS AND THE WAY OUT

VII   The "Crisis of Democracy"

The fascist movement built on petty bourgeois ideology and brought together largely déclassé elements of the middle classes in its combat organisations. It developed in this form in almost all the advanced capitalist countries. It surfaced nearly everywhere in the period of crisis following the first world war, and in the crisis of 1929 onwards. But only in Italy and Germany did it become a decisive political factor. It seized power as the "political solution" to the postwar crisis in Italy and to the crisis of the great depression in Germany. Why was it able to become a decisive factor in precisely these countries, and why was it that the Italian and German bourgeoisies did not or could not find any other way out of the crisis?

Bourgeois theoreticians often try to deduce the rise of fascist rule from the "crisis of mass democracy". In a book published in 1929 which analyses Italian fascism,[30] Hermann Heller attempted to make a theoretical generalistion of the problem of fascism. Both his conclusion and his theoretical premises, in what is a descriptive sociological analysis, can be summed up as saying that the universally accepted order of values which characterises all democracies was on its way to dissolution:

> "Without a community of political values there is neither a community of political will nor a legal community. The deepest roots of the political crisis in Europe are hidden in the dissolution of this community of values."[31]

Heller assumes that the dissolution of the community of values was already manifest in nineteenth-century (liberal and socialist) rationalism. This rationalism, with its "scientific" laws which could be discovered by scientific means and which allegedly determine the predictable path of social progress, and "with its idea of the constitutional state", was based "on a substantial ideal of that which is just"; but it already implied a latent negation of every value. The ultimate statement of rationalism is that "the whole of life is nothing but a sociological problem devoid of meaning and value content, and while the world of the human animal

51

creates religious, metaphysical and moral illusions, it in fact only obeys laws which are devoid of any reason or sense."[32] Bourgeois rationalism was simply the veil drawn over the bourgeoisie's disillusion; at a certain point it necessarily turned into its opposite, into an ideology which openly declared that every political objective is an expression of the aims of those who possess power, and that faith in the "rationality" or "rationalisability" of social processes is the power-instrument of those who possess power. According to Hermann Heller, this turning-point in the development of bourgeois rationalism came with Pareto's sociology:

> "Pareto's doctrine of ideology . . . represents the point where the rational idea of social law turns into its opposite and negates itself, leading politically to the most radical disillusionment possible. Not only every utopia but every political programme, every ideal and every objective become entirely meaningless if they are not regarded as the technical instrument of the application of violence. . . . Pareto's allegedly mathematical sociology is quite simply the neomachiavellianism of the disillusioned bourgeoisie."[33]

At the same time, the reaction against modern bourgeois mass democracy with its corporative and syndicalist ideas has also, like every community of values which lacks a generally accepted scale of values, turned into its opposite:

> "The corporative idea must, out of inner necessity, turn into its exact opposite, into the least organic but necessarily centralised dictatorship, lacking any organic continuity, to the extent that it does not possess a static and sociologically effective cosmos of values."[34]

According to Heller, the self-destruction of bourgeois rationalism (Pareto) and organic activism lacking any stable or concrete value content (Sorel) supplied the common, converging roots of Italian fascism. He is quite justified in emphasising the fact (which in Mussolini's case is absolutely clear) that "with the exception of the formal ideology of violence, there is in reality not one single idea which could connect the fascism of 1920 or 1915 with that of 1922 or 1929".[35] The dissolution of any kind of community of values necessarily led to the crisis of democracy:

> "In reality, I limit myself to the spiritual-'phraseological' confirmation of my political will; I subordinate my own convictions to the will of the majority only if I estimate the

52

concrete community of will and values of the totality to be politically superior (even this superiority is judged to be, in ethical or religious terms, a relative one) to the actual realisation of my better judgement."[36]

There is a lot of truth in the way Hermann Heller thinks. His analysis is nevertheless problematical, because he regards the existence or dissolution of the "community of values" (the spirit of the *Geisteswissenschaften*) as a kind of spontaneous process, and interprets the problem of fascism as a projection of this immanent spiritual dynamic on to the plane of political organisation, of the "formation of the political will". According to him, from the moment bourgeois society is born a process has begun by which the egoistic material interests gain the upper hand over the traditional community of values, and this is gradually recognised and accepted as a fact by the bourgeoisie. He fails to realise that the materialism of the bourgeois and the idealism of the "citizen" necessarily complement each other, and that therefore it is only those processes which exist at the deeper levels of society, hidden behind the ideological-political domain, that can and do force the bourgeoisie to temporarily negate its self-created values and to openly recognise the totality of its selfish material interests as the motivating force of its own society. Unless the deeper economic processes and corresponding social structures are analysed, fascism cannot be "deduced" from the crisis of democracy as a form of rule or political institution.

This has to be emphasised, for it is not only bourgeois theoreticians who make this mistake. The standpoint which the communists adopted conceals a similar mistake. When the Comintern, at its seventh congress, described the specific difference of fascism as being its "anti-democratic nature", this meant (for there was still no *concrete* class analysis) that the essence of fascism lay in the fact that it was a kind of anti-democratic capitalism, a form of bourgeois rule in which the bourgeoisie was "already" forced to repudiate the democratic ideals which it had been proclaiming for several centuries. It is a well-known fact that until 1935 the stalinist leadership of the International did not make any distinction between the democratic and fascist forms of capitalism. The situation changed after 1935, but the concrete class movements which lay behind the fascist form of rule remained unanalysed. In these circumstances, Trotsky was justified in asking:

"Is there any difference in the 'class content' of these two régimes [bourgeois democracy and fascism]? If we pose the question merely in terms of the *ruling* class, then there is no difference at all. But if we examine the situation and the relationships between *all* classes from the standpoint of the proletariat, then the difference seems to be very important."[37]

If like the Comintern in 1935 one distinguishes between democracy and fascism without examining the concrete situation and the relation between all the classes, then in the last analysis one's ideas are based, just like those of the bourgeois theories which set out from the idea of the crisis of democracy, on the premise of a difference in transcendent values.

Of course, it would be ridiculous to assert that the seizure of power by fascism had no connection with the crisis of democracy. The democratic form of rule was in crisis both in Italy and in Germany. But this does not explain how fascism came to seize power. The question is, more precisely, *why* was democracy in crisis?

It should first of all be firmly emphasised that there is no sense in speaking about the crisis of bourgeois democracy in general. There is no characteristic tendency in the history of bourgeois society that leads from democracy to dictatorship, as is suggested by Herman Heller and by other bourgeois theoreticians, as well as by the communist movement of the period (i.e. that the general crisis of capitalism would force the bourgeoisie to gradually remove its democratic mask and exercise its power in an openly terrorist manner). It is superfluous to point out that fascism is not the first terrorist form of political rule in the history of bourgeois society, or that both in the fascist period and today democracy is a *functioning* political structure in the majority of capitalist countries. We know, of course, that this is only "pseudo-democracy", i.e. it is based not "only" on material inequalities but also on basic social and political ones (it allows only a restricted layer to participate in decision-making on the important social issues). But there has never been any place or period in which bourgeois democracy has got rid of these inequalities.

Consequently, not only are the bourgeois theories (which account for the developing crisis of democracy by the dissolution of the "political community of values") and the seemingly opposed pseudo-marxist ideas both incapable of explaining the development of fascism, but so are those marxist ideas which try to deduce the fascisation of politics directly from the transformation of capitalism's economic structure.

All these theories, including their "marxist" variants, take as their point of departure an essentially static theoretical model of capitalism. They explain the *functional* disturbances of the capitalist system in the twentieth century as the *final* intensification of its inner contradictions, the "general crisis" of the system; the bourgeoisie may find a temporary way out of these difficulties by resorting to extreme violence against the proletariat, which has become increasingly dissatisfied and, moreover, revolutionary as a result of the intensification of the contradictions. But they think the bourgeoisie is incapable of restoring the conditions for the "normal" functioning of the system. However, this description contradicts the facts — even on the surface. For there has never been a single case, regardless of what the serious crises of the system actually indicated, of fascism conquering power immediately as the result of a threatening revolutionary situation.

There have been marxists who could already see in the fascist period that capitalism did have a way out of the crisis of the first world war and the great depression, and that the development of monopoly capitalism had not yet led bourgeois society into a dead-end. But the authors of these theories usually maintained that fascism was the *sole* adequate political form for the new phase of capitalist development. Their theory apparently does not differ much from the one mentioned earlier. What is really common to these two theories (i.e. their common mistake) is that they could no longer see a *democratic* way out of the crisis for capitalism. They have simply interpreted the role of the anti-democratic "fascisation" solution in different ways. The Comintern's theory was that the existence of the fascist movement and of fascist dictatorship was an *indication* of the crisis; the latter theories saw fascism as the *solution* of the crisis, a political system which did not temporarily delay the overthrow of capitalism but ensured an adequate framework for its further development.

There was certainly more truth in this second train of thought. Of course, it proved later to be the case that there was a democratic political structure, containing many new aspects, which turned out to be compatible with the changes taking place in the structure of capitalism; and it also became clear that the *process*

55

of transformation itself did not necessarily have to be accompanied by a temporary fascist or semi-fascist type of political system. But what cannot be denied is that capitalism did not get stuck in a permanent crisis, and that in Germany it was in fact the period of nazi rule that created the conditions for the neo-capitalist structure to function after nazi rule itself had been destroyed. And incidentally, as we shall see briefly later, it is not exactly true to say that the transformation could have occurred without the intermediary episode of fascist rule: the second world war, initiated by fascist Germany, made a considerable contribution to the success of the democratic version of the transformation, particularly in the USA with the New Deal.

One of those who held the second viewpoint was Karl Korsch, whose ideas may be summarised as follows. The old capitalist system based on laissez-faire got itself and its huge political and ideological superstructure into a chronic crisis. It seemed that there was no other solution than proletarian revolution. The historic new events of the two decades after the world war, however, showed that a different kind of outcome was possible. A new type of capitalist society developed which could no longer accommodate the democratic and peaceful conduct of traditional socialists and trade unionists. The changeover was effected by a counter-revolutionary and anti-proletarian movement which was, nevertheless, objectively progressive and had an anti-capitalistic and plebeian ideology; it even used the unrestrained methods developed by the preceding revolution in order to achieve its own limited aims. It was clear that capitalist society had not yet reached its final historical limits, and that neither the ruling classes nor the reformist socialists had reached the limits of their own possibilities for development. The period of democratic reforms was followed by another phase of development, the phase of fascist transformation, which was revolutionary in its political form but evolutionary in its objective social content.[38]

We can see that according to Korsch, the evolutionary phase of capitalism, during which it based itself on the direct political rule of the bourgeoisie and on the integration of reformist socialism, had come to its final end. We know today that he was fundamentally wrong. His mistake was probably fuelled by the fact that in 1940, when he was writing, the success of the New Deal still seemed to be in doubt (the number of fully unemployed in the

USA was still running at eight million, or fifteen per cent of the working population, while fascist Germany already had full employment by 1937). This mistake had negative effects on his political stance. Because he thought that fascism was the only possible way out for capitalism, he regarded all ideas of a united anti-fascist front under any form as completely senseless. For him, anti-fascism was absolutely identical with anti-capitalism, and the only possible form of anti-fascism was proletarian revolutionary practice. Of course, one could see very little of the final consequences of nazism from the USA in 1940, and it is clear from Korsch's analysis that he did not in fact see them. He wrote at the time: "As far as the workers are concerned, they have only exchanged one form of serfdom for another."[39] If he was wrong in this, however, he was not wrong in his view that it was the job of fascist dictatorship to carry out fundamental changes in the structure of capitalism, even though he did not see that these changes could also take place under other forms of rule and in different socio-political conditions.

To sum up my viewpoint so far, fascism can only be understood if we examine it in close relation to the basic changes which occurred everywhere in the structure of the capitalist system in the twentieth century (and essentially between the outbreak of the first world war and the end of the second). It is nevertheless impossible to "explain" fascism by means of these changes alone, or to deduce it from them. In order for fascism to arise, the socio-economic processes had to find their specific political structures.

VIII The Crisis of Liberal Capitalism

The whole structure of capitalism, its economic mechanism and its corresponding social structure, has been transformed in the twentieth century. This transformation was preceded and in fact caused by the deep crisis of the "classical", liberalistic form of capitalism which was based on the "automatic regulator" of the free market. In the first years and decades of this century many important marxist theoreticians — Hilferding, Kautsky, Lenin and Luxemburg among them — noted the changes which were occurring in the economic structure of capitalism and demonstrated that capitalism had reached a new phase of development. But during this period, the marxist analysts of imperialism thought (in different ways, according to their political standpoint) that the new phase of capitalism was a period of intensification of its contradictions, and that it would be immediately followed by the turn to socialism. They did not see it as a further historical period of capitalist evolution.

The fact that Kautsky and Lenin interpreted the situated in different ways is irrelevant to our argument. According to Kautsky, the increasing trend to monopolisation was going to lead almost automatically to the self-abolition of the capitalist system. Lenin, on the other hand, maintained that the situation of permanent crisis which imperialism had created furnished only the *possibility* that proletarian revolution might bring about socialist transformation. For us today, the essential point is simply that in this period, marxists recognised the trend towards monopolisation and saw that this would mean the capitalist economy and the bourgeois state becoming much more closely entwined than they had been in the preceding "classical" phase of development, but that they did not see the bourgeois state being capable, little by little, of actually regulating the economy. Unconsciously at first, but later much more consciously, the bourgeois state sought and found the means with which to prevent or eliminate economic crises (which until then had appeared in the form of natural catastrophes) without removing the basic features of the capitalist system itself.

In that period it was difficult to foresee this. It is true, of course, that during the first world war (which with its horrifying sacrifices of men and material was the first serious sign of basic functional disturbances in the system) the various capitalist states introduced a number of emergency measures which already made it impossible to speak of the free capitalist market as an automatic regulator. But it was not only marxists but the bourgeois economists and politicians too who saw these interventions as merely temporary affairs, which could be explained or excused by the extraordinary circumstances and which would have to be dismantled at the end of the war, so that the capitalist economy could function "normally" again. And this is in fact what happened during the years after the war. However, the automatic functioning of the economy (of course, the only time it had ever been "automatic" was in the heads of liberal economists) proved impossible to restore. One of the most important aspects of this was the progressive but quite rapid weakening of the international character of capital (the United States, for example, suspended immigration at this point). It was also typical of this period that the regulations of the Versailles treaty expressly affected the *functioning* of the German economy: the victors not only demanded reparations from the vanquished, but also interfered directly in their economic development.

It was still difficult to see, even at this stage, that these changes in the international relations of capital and the transformations in the structure of the economy from around the turn of the century would demand that the wartime emergency measures be permanently instituted. Like the marxists, the bourgeois economists and politicians believed a "planned" capitalist economic system, ignoring the "natural laws" of production, to be inconceivable.[40] But while the bourgeois economists and politicians hoped that the world war and postwar crisis were only minor functional disturbances in a basically well-functioning system and would not necessarily recur, the marxists were certain that things would *necessarily* develop in the direction of socialism. According to the revolutionaries, the inevitably recurring crises would shake capitalism to its foundations; according to the reformists, it would somehow be possible to free the capitalist economy of its functional disturbances, but this would then no longer be capitalism — society would grow peacefully into socialism.

Of course, there was one respect in which the world economic crisis that broke out in 1929 did confirm the revolutionary marxists' theory: it proved that the first world war was not just one accidental episode in the history of liberal capitalism. However, the crisis did not turn out to prove the non-viability of capitalism as such, but only that of the liberal model. In the decades after the crisis a worldwide change took place and the neo-capitalist system emerged, whose basic characteristic is that the capitalist state intervenes in the functioning of the economic system; it does not do so temporarily, in order to dispose of the threatening or already present crisis, but guides the economy permanently. The limits of this analysis prevent me from dealing in detail with the reasons why the liberal system went bankrupt, and I can only sketch in the economic background to the process. (I am indebted here to Ferenc Jánossy.)

The extensive growth of the capitalist mode of production had come to an end (in other words, the entire economy had become capitalist) in England by the mid-nineteenth century and in the other developed capitalist countries (the USA, Germany, France, Switzerland, Belgium, Holland, Denmark, Norway, Sweden) by the beginning of the twentieth century. This meant first of all that economic progress could no longer be based on the introduction of manpower into the capitalist sector from the non-capitalist parts of the economy, and secondly that the only place where increasing production could find new markets was among the workers and employees working within capitalist production. (Permanent arms production is another "solution" — but only a temporary one, as we shall see in the next chapter.) Therefore it became one of the basic prerequisites of the maintenance of capitalism (and therefore of the vital interests of the capitalist class) that the proletariat and the other strata who lived off wages and salaries should constantly be creating and presenting effective demand for the goods produced by the national capital. The basic function of the capitalist state was now to create the political means with which to secure the increasing satisfaction of the particular needs of these strata, and even to try and arouse needs artificially so as to have a continuous production of new effective demand.

The securing of effective demand for consumer goods is only one element in the guiding economic function of the modern capitalist state. The state plays an incomparably greater part in the economy in a direct way, partly by financing the huge enterprises which produce a considerable percentage of the national income, and partly by influencing private enterprise with its financial and credit policies.

We shall see later how the two great attempts at eliminating the world crisis within national boundaries — Roosevelt's New Deal on the one hand (the classic example of how to achieve state guidance of the economy within the framework of a manipulated democracy) and German national socialism on the other — were both based on the two elements outlined above. But the balance between the two elements differed, precisely because of the decisively different nature of their political structures. This difference was not simply a divergence between the respective political systems which carried out the economic transition, but was also in many respects a determining factor in their political perspectives. Although the nazi régime in Germany carried out its task of restructuring the economy within the capitalist system, a task which was on the agenda all over the world, nevertheless its own brand of solution led to "pure" economic consequences which caused the system to live in a permanence of political tension, the tension between the already established basis of the neo-capitalist structure and the fascist political superstructure made consolidation impossible.

IX Fascism as the Only Alternative (Italy)

So far we have been looking exclusively at German national social-ism and its function. In spite of the basic identity between the forms of rule and the political means used by the two régimes, Italian fascism performed a different historical function from nazism. It was only the growth of national socialism in particu-lar into a mass movement, and its seizure of power, that turned fascism into a phenomenon of world-historical importance. If fascism had only gained power in Italy, then today it would al-ready be an unimportant episode in European history. It is clear that the importance of Italian fascism grew retrospectively, as a result of the successes of nazism. Its retrospective importance lies firstly in the fact that Mussolini's movement was the first success-ful rightist mass movement to appear in a revolutionary disguise in the twentieth century, and Hitler and his cohorts learned a lot from Mussolini. Secondly, an analysis of the history of Italian fascism can help us enormously to clarify the specific *political* conditions which, by meeting the economic needs, resulted in the fascist transition to a neo-capitalist structure.

Italian and German economic conditions certainly differed. Ger-many was one of the most developed capitalist powers in the world, while Italy was a very underdeveloped capitalist country when the fascists seized power. But the common or at least simi-lar features in the political structure of the two countries, and in their postwar political history, were just as numerous as the economic differences. It should simply be noted that politically the bourgeoisie in both countries (for different reasons) was un-organised and weak, incapable of governing. The Italian bour-geoisie, however, was weak in the economic sense too, and because it was unable to secure political rule for itself it was unable to create the conditions for the development of capitalism either.

The period of extensive growth of the capitalist economy was far from finished in Italy by the end of the first world war. In fact it had only just started. The task of Italian fascism was precisely to secure the extensive growth (i.e. the conditions for the accumulation of capital) of which Italian bourgeois democracy had proved to be entirely incapable. To my knowledge it was Gramsci who first elucidated the historical origins of the specific features of the Italian situation. Franz Borkenau, on whose excellent study[41] I have in many respects relied, made an analysis of the same problem which turns out to be unanimous with Gramsci's, although it was probably completely independent of the latter.

As a result of the fight for national unity, a bourgeois parliamentary system was set up in Italy in the 1860s. But the big feudal estates still had a decisive impact on the Italian economy, and so the conservative landowner class also had a large amount of political power. The political system was based on an alliance between feudal landowners and capitalists, and this hindered the progress of capitalist development and industrialisation. If the bourgeoisie did not want to be economically at the mercy of the landowning aristocracy, it had to create new political conditions.

While the bourgeoisie was still feeble it helped to develop the labour movement, so that it could rely on the movement in turn to help force the landowning class out of political power. It was nothing new, of course, for the bourgeoisie to look to the "fourth estate" for support in taking power from the feudal landowners. What was quite new and unique was the fact that it relied on the workers' *organised class movement* and even encouraged its development. According to Gramsci, "in no country was the rise and development of trade unions and co-operatives assisted to the same extent as in Italy."[42] But this had peculiar consequences for both bourgeoisie and proletariat. From 1900 onwards (when the compromise between the bourgeoisie and the feudal landowners dissolved), Giolitti's policies favoured the proletariat and formed the basis of the Italian liberal democratic system. It appears as if it were the prototype of modern manipulative capitalism, relying on social democracy and its mass influence. But one of the most essential preconditions for this kind of power-structure was entirely missing in Italy: the complete capitalisation of the economy, an abundance of commodities, and workers sufficiently well-off to buy them. Only part of the country (the Turin region) was industrialised, and only a small part of agricultural production (in Emilia and the Po Valley) was actually capable of standing up to competition. The result was that the satisfaction of the workers' demands, which were voiced by the artificially

63

strengthened trade-union movement but which nevertheless had to be satisfied because of the movement's real strength, clashed not only with certain private capitalist interests as in the present capitalist systems, but also with the sum total of interests of the capitalist class as a class. The politically integrated, reformist labour movement actually threatened capitalist interests. The only reason why the capitalists refrained from upsetting the compromise was because they were still not strong enough, and such a step would have thrown them at the mercy of the feudal landowners once more. But on the other hand, their satisfaction of trade-union demands hindered the process of capitalist accumulation, made it impossible to modernise the country's economic structure, and completely ruined the petty bourgeois layers without offering them the opportunity to find work in industry.

In economic terms, therefore, Italian reformism fulfilled an expressly reactionary function: it hindered the development of the economy. This is precisely why the compromise eventually became untenable for the working class too, since it could only have been integrated in a relatively lasting sense if production had been in continual expansion. (It was this that determined the leftist attitudes of the majority of Italian socialists, although the trade-union bureaucracy itself and the wing of the party linked to this bureaucracy, as well as its parliamentary faction, followed the majority of European social democrat leaders.) There was a clear demonstration of this in 1919 and 1920, when the working class tried to seize *economic* power: at the time, this was unique in the entire European labour movement. But precisely because the policy of Giolittism was to secure for the working class the greatest possible political influence within the limits of liberal parliamentary democracy, the relatively left-wing leaders of the labour movement did not realise the importance of political power. The Italian left socialists understood better than anyone how fundamentally important economic power and democracy at the point of production were for the working class, but there were only a few among them who, like Gramsci, saw clearly that "the complete abolition of parliamentary democracy is also a necessary precondition for the revolution in Italy".[43] As a result of this, the revolutionary attempt of 1920 failed (and failed without a shot being fired), although five hundred large enterprises including the most important ones were under the control of the workers' councils, and in Emilia the village proletarian organisations were dictating conditions to the landowners. The Socialist Party did not take a single step towards seizing political power, or to be more precise, it wanted to obtain it in the parliamentary manner. Ultimately a situation arose in which the working class still seemed to be unwilling to take power, while the bourgeoisie in spite of this remained completely helpless, sank into apathy and could see no escape at all.

The solution was provided for them, by Mussolini's *squadri d'azione*, the masses of armed petty bourgeois who (not entirely without justification) held the workers responsible for their misery, those workers who had obtained some economic benefits as a result of struggle. They turned against the organisations of the proletariat and began to demoralise and destroy them by violence; it was no coincidence that they started with the communes of Emilia, which still held economic power in their hands. This came as a godsend to the ruling classes (both the bourgeoisie and the liberal landowners of the north), who until that point had had no perspective. They supported Mussolini's annihilation of the labour organisations without the slightest intention of helping the fascists take power. But from the very moment that Mussolini's storm-troopers (with the help of the bourgeois state) became stronger than the workers' organisations, the weak liberal bourgeoisie was once again faced with a dilemma: either they could enter an alliance with the southern feudal landowners again, or with Mussolini. The first choice would mean a share in political power along with the feudal landlords, but with the latter thwarting the growth of their economic power and hampering vigorous capital accumulation. It would make the creation of a modern Italy impossible. The alliance with Mussolini, on the other hand, would mean that the haute bourgeoisie would have to renounce political power, but that it would now be able to increase its economic power at a vigorous rate, and that a path would open towards capital accumulation. Faced with these two alternatives, the bourgeoisie was never in doubt about its choice.

The specific structure of the country, therefore, played a decisive role in the Italian bourgeoisie's choice of fascism. It was basically an underdeveloped agricultural country which had not yet become capitalised, but which nevertheless had a well-developed labour movement.

It goes without saying that the revolutionary crisis of 1918 to 1920 also offered Italy the fully progressive alternative of a socialist Italy. But a socialist Italy would also have been unable to satisfy the particular needs of the proletariat, even at the level achieved by the reformist labour movement in the first two decades of the century (these reformist achievements actually constituted a serious obstacle to the economic development of the country). A socialist government could, of course, have distributed the burdens of capital accumulation "fairly", unlike the fascist government. But because "the socialist revolution proved to be unsuccessful, so — as long as we do not consider it a solution if the country sinks into social chaos and thus back to an earlier level of development, the level of Spain — there was no other solution left than the development of a national capitalism adapting itself completely to the latest requirements; this is precisely what fascism did".[44] Because the socialist alternative, as a result of the proletarian movement's immaturity and unpreparedness, had been objectively discarded, fascism was the only progressive solution that remained from the point of view of Italian economic development. This has to be said, in spite of all the horrors that went with it (which in any case cannot be compared to those of nazism).

It is a well-known fact that during the period of fascist rule Italy set out towards rapid capitalisation. The country was electrified, developed motor and artificial silk industries were set up, an up-to-date banking system was created, agriculture thrived, substantial agricultural areas were created by draining the marshlands, an important highway network was built, etc. The rapid progress of Italy after the second world war, and the fact that now it is already on the way to intensive capitalist development, would have been inconceivable were it not for the social processes launched in the fascist period.

When Karl Korsch described fascism as a progressive alternative springing from a situation where the proletarian revolution had failed to come about, it was obviously this Italian process that he had in mind. But no conclusion at all can be drawn from the history of Italian fascism that will apply equally to the function of German fascism, in spite of the numerous analogous elements in the *political* situation of the two countries: namely a powerful proletarian movement, a *politically* feeble bourgeoisie, an unequivocally revolutionary situation after the war followed by an aborted revolution. The progressive function of Italian fascism consisted in the capitalisation of the economy. German fascism could not have fulfilled this function, for between the wars it was already the third-ranking capitalist power in the world.

X Fascism as One Alternative (Germany)

Many people attributed identical functions to Italian fascism and German national socialism in the fascist era, and still do so. Both seized power in political circumstances which were in many respects similar, both relied on a rightist mass movement which displayed anti-capitalist features, and both came about *not* in a period of revolutionary crisis threatening capitalism but after this period was over, at a point when the crisis could no longer be solved in a revolutionary way. In addition to this, the political system set up after the victory demonstrated essentially similar features in the two countries. Without threatening capitalist private property in the least, it put into the strongholds of politics a stratum which until then had only figured as the political opponent of the régime. The political power of this stratum was both extensively and intensively much greater than that of the politicians whom it replaced in the régime. Extensively because the fascist party became, within a year or two in Italy and within a month or two in Germany, the sole omnipotent political organisation in the country, the possessor of an executive power unrestricted by any kind of legal limits. Intensively because the régime completely politicised all those spheres of life which had until then been completely free of political influence, or had at least appeared to be so. And it was the principal characteristic of both régimes (I am emphasising here the aspect which can be considered fundamental for marxist theory) that they removed all the independent mass organisations of the proletariat in the most drastic way. They removed not only those which aimed at the revolutionary overthrow of the capitalist system (i.e. not only the communist parties) but also the mass reformist organisations which had until then formed an integral part of the system; not only those of an explicitly political nature (the Italian Socialist Party and the German Social Democratic Party) but also the economic organisations, i.e. the trade unions.

This latter feature was indispensable for Italian fascism's fulfilment of its historical function. The same thing happened in

Germany too, but it certainly does not follow from this that the nazi régime assisted in the process of capital accumulation. I shall try to analyse in detail the connection between nazi political rule and the German capitalist economy in the next chapter. Here I will simply try to answer the following question: what forced the bourgeoisie to renounce direct political rule in favour of fascism?

Developed German capitalism had no economic worries about the landed aristocracy, who were already capitalised (albeit "Prussian-style"). The class compromise effected in Bismarck's and Wilhelm's Germany created the conditions for rapid capitalisation, as opposed to the Italian class compromise in the period between the Risorgimento and Umberto's assassination. It would therefore not have been disadvantageous in the least for the German bourgeoisie if a political system based on a landowner-capitalist compromise, in the form of a monarchy, had been restored.

The alliance which the German bourgeoisie reached with the reformist labour movement in the course of the 1918 revolution could also have remained acceptable to it. The economic prosperity which existed between 1924 and 1929 shows that the conditions for a political system based on integrating the reformist labour movement and satisfying its demands were already ripe in Germany. In this period a lot of social reforms were introduced in Germany which in the USA were only carried out under the New Deal. (These measures were certainly a heavy burden for the middle classes, but they did not hinder the industrial development of capitalism.) Consequently, fascism was far from being the sole possibility for capitalism's economic development. It is true, of course, that in fascist Germany a lot of changes were made in the economic structure which, as it turned out in the postwar period, were very conducive to further economic development. But even if we assume that these structural changes could only be carried out by capitalist rule (which is far from being the case), it was not the possibility of economic development in general that was at stake in Germany as it was in Italy.

As far as the *economic* situation of Germany was concerned, there was a choice between democracy and fascism. Just before the fascist seizure of power in Germany, Trotsky very vehemently raised the possibility that bourgeois rule had a choice between social democracy and fascism. In January 1932 he argued against

69

the resolution of the Comintern's Executive Committee which declared fascism and democracy to be identical:

"A contradiction exists between democracy and fascism. This contradiction is not at all 'absolute' nor, in the language of marxism, does it mean the opposition of two different classes. It concerns different systems of rule by one and the same class. These two systems, parliamentary democracy and fascism, rely on different combinations of the oppressed and exploited classes, and inevitably clash sharply with each other.

"Social democracy, which is today the principal representative of the bourgeois parliamentary régime, relies on the workers, and fascism on the petty bourgeoisie. Social democracy can have no influence without the mass workers' organisations, and fascism on the other hand cannot consolidate its power without destroying the workers' organisations. The basic operational area for social democracy is parliament; the fascist system is based on the destruction of parliamentarism. As far as the monopoly bourgeoisie is concerned, the parliamentary and the fascist systems are simply two different ways of ruling: it chooses one or the other according to the historical circumstances. But as far as social democracy and fascism are concerned, the choice of one instrument or the other is of fundamental importance; for them, it is a question of political life or death. . . . Democracy is just as much of a bourgeois nature as fascism is . . . but the ruling class does not move in a vacuum. It is always related somehow to the other classes. In the 'democratic' régimes of the advanced capitalist society, the bourgeoisie relies primarily on the fact that the working class is tamed by the reformists. We find the most developed form of this system in England, where it is represented by both the Labour and the Conservative government. In the fascist system, at least in its first stage of development, capital relies on the petty bourgeoisie, which destroys the organisations of the proletariat."[45]

It is clear, then, that Trotsky had already realised in 1932 that these were the two given alternatives by which monopoly capitalism could maintain its own rule. He did not raise the question of the historical circumstances under which the bourgeoisie prefers one or the other form of rule. But his analysis dealt with the German situation in the moments before the nazi seizure of power, when it was already quite clear both that the bourgeoisie was giving a free rein to fascism's development as a mass movement, and that it would not stand up to fascism (whether it could have done or not was immaterial at that point). And therefore it was impossible for Trotsky to formulate the question from a historical perspective, as could be done now or, indeed, before 1930 when the German bourgeoisie had not yet taken any decision about the solution. In the Germany of 1932, there was only one way of stating the situation from the point of view of the proletariat: the bourgeoisie was making it possible for fascism to seize power, and this seizure of power was imminent. It was in the vital interests of the proletariat to prevent this. The only *open* question from the proletariat's point of view, therefore, was the following: is it possible to create a united workers' front to resist fascism and thus to force the bourgeoisie into revising its decision, under the threat of being involved in a civil war? In other words: is it possible to convince the masses of social democrat workers that fascism threatens their own narrowly conceived class interests, and to convince the communists that, at such a point, any compromise is acceptable as long as it prevents a fascist seizure of power? The bourgeoisie had already taken its own decision: from the standpoint of practical politics, therefore, it was senseless to enquire whether the bourgeoisie originally had any alternatives or not or, if it had, what forced it to choose the fascist solution from among them. It was only the proletariat that still had alternatives to choose from.

Even in 1930 Trotsky had already raised questions about the causes of the fascist advance in Italy, and attempted to draw conclusions from this for the benefit of the policy to be followed in Germany. He reached the conclusion that the "missed or unexploited revolutionary situation" had led to the victory of fascism (and subsequently to its emergence in Germany), that the victory of fascism was the result of a revolutionary situation in which "the vanguard of the proletariat demonstrated its inability to change the fate of all classes (including the petty bourgeoisie) as the leading force of the nation".[46] Trotsky thus opposed the Comintern view that the birth of fascism was conditioned by the strength of the proletarian revolutionary movement and by the bourgeoisie's fear of a takeover of power by the proletariat. It was obvious that in both Italy and Germany, fascism advanced at a time when it was already clear that the revolutionary opening had been missed.

Many writers conclude from this that the emergence, consolidation and victory of fascism was conditioned by the strength of the reformist rather than the revolutionary labour movement. Otto Bauer, for example, writes as follows:

"Fascism did not triumph at the moment when the bourgeoisie was threatened by proletarian revolution. It triumphed when the proletariat had already lost its strength and was forced on to the defensive, when the tide of revolution was ebbing. The capitalist and landowning classes did not surrender state power to the fascist stormtroopers in order to defend themselves against a threatening proletarian revolution, but with the intention of pressing down wages, obliterating the gains of the working class, destroying the trade unions and the political power of the working class: in other words, not in order to suppress revolutionary socialism but in order to destroy the achievements of reformist socialism."[47]

Ignazio Silone puts forward an even more extreme version of the same view (he only analyses Italian fascism, and his general conclusions are in many ways justified as far as Italy is concerned, but they cannot be applied to nazism):

"The loud-mouthed revolutionism of the maximalists only threatens the bulbs in the street lamps and sometimes the bones of a few police spies. But reformism, with its co-operatives, its ability to increase the workers' incomes even at times of crisis and its support of the unemployed, threatens something much more sacred: capitalist profit. . . . Capitalism defends itself against the maximalists (who in any case spend all their time singing 'Bandiera Rossa' and 'The International') with the aid of the law, and if the old laws are not enough it creates new ones; but against reformism, which disturbs the equilibrium between the classes in a peaceful, democratic and lawful way, capitalism turns bloodthirsty and starts using fascist gangs. . . . Reformism is not dangerous as long as it is weak but only when it has gained strength, i.e. when it has reached the limit beyond which democracy and legality may be used against capitalist profit."[48]

It is clear from these quotations that there are decisive differences between the two extremes of Trotsky and Silone. But all three writers quoted above have a common point of departure. This consists in their view that the bourgeoisie does *not* support fascism, help it to emerge or to seize power in periods when the revolutionary labour movement is strong. Indeed, it is a fact that in neither of the two countries did a significant fascist movement exist during the ascending phase of the revolution. But there is a decisive difference between the view that fascism is brought about by an unexploited (and, from a given moment, unexploitable) revolutionary situation and the view that it emerges because of the strength of the reformist movement. The latter view is quite unacceptable. First of all, the existence of a strong reformist labour movement capable of enforcing its demands does not lead the bourgeoisie to support fascism (what about Britain?). Secondly, the transition to a neo-capitalist structure demands precisely the existence of powerful reformist workers' organisations (one of the basic factors in the American New Deal was the strengthening of the trade unions).

But the "unexploited revolutionary situation" is an inadequate answer too. Although German fascism emerged during the revolutionary period of crisis immediately after the war, it did not become a real mass movement or an actual power factor until the 1929 crisis, when there was no revolutionary situation at all. There is no doubt, of course, that fascism has always advanced together with some social crisis, and that it has always exploited some kind of mass dissatisfaction. But it is impossible to lay down any kind of general "formula" by which the fascist threat can be "calculated" from the data at our disposal. Each concrete case of fascism becoming a mass movement and seizing power can only be explained by the totality of the social situation in that particular country and by the whole complex of economic, social and political evidence.

Those capitalist countries that had entered the stage of intensive development did in fact have the alternative which Trotsky mentioned. Therefore, in view of Germany's level of economic development, it existed concretely there too. One cannot explain why the German bourgeoisie "chose" the fascist alternative by analysing the specific features of the development of capitalism in Germany — or at least, this explanation is insufficient. The answer must be sought first of all in the German *political* situation. Further economic development, remaining within the framework of bourgeois political rule and relying on a reformist labour movement, would certainly have been possible in Germany. It was "only" the political preconditions for this development that were lacking.

Consequently, to have opposed German fascism from the standpoint of some other prospect than that of immediate proletarian revolution would not have been mere ineffective moralising. In Italy, the alternative between bourgeois democracy and fascism was an alternative between economic stagnation, even decline, and economic development; therefore any defence of democracy against fascism was reactionary unless it was undertaken from the standpoint of proletarian democracy. But in Germany the level of economic development *in itself* would have made the transition to the neo-capitalist system possible within the framework of bourgeois democracy. And if such an alternative exists, then the class interest of the proletariat undoubtedly lies in realising this possibility as against the possibility of fascist rule. It is impossible to agree with the view that it is irrelevant for the proletariat what form of bourgeois class rule it has to contend with. (We should recall here the well-known fact that the Comintern held this view until 1934-5, and that even then it only revised its opinion out of mere tactical considerations. It was a view also put forward by some of the representatives of the marxist left opposition, such as Korsch.)

There are two fundamental reasons why it is possible and necessary for the proletariat to distinguish between the two alternatives. First of all, the proletariat's class interests (in the narrower sense of the word) call for it to choose democracy. It is true that the democratic variant of the neo-capitalist structure relies on the reformist labour movement being integrated into the system, and that this is, in the immediate, a clear hindrance to the overall development of proletarian class consciousness. But the reformist organisations are nevertheless *independent* workers' organisations, they are *class* organisations (in contrast to the fascist corporations), and in favourable circumstances they can form the basis for the development of revolutionary proletarian consciousness. It is not irrelevant for the proletariat, moreover, that the democratic variant of the neo-capitalist structure offers the highest working-class living standards possible within the framework of the capitalist system, therefore opening up the broadest possible educational opportunities for it; it has always been the developed rather than the backward sections of workers who constitute the real social basis for the formation of revolutionary class consciousness.

The second consideration which makes the choice of alternatives necessary transcends the question of immediate proletarian class interests. Although the immediate objective of the proletarian revolution is to create the class dictatorship of the proletariat, this latter is simply a means for creating a society free from alienation, a society which eliminates the gap between essence and existence and thus gives every individual the opportunity for the widest possible mastery over the values which have been formed in the course of development of the human species. In this respect the democratic variant of the neo-capitalist structure is not a step forward. But at least it maintains the validity of those values — which in reality the majority of individuals are unable to realise — as an ideal, whereas the ideology of fascism is built on the negation of nearly all bourgeois society's ideal values. The triumph of fascism, whose ideology is always adopted by broad sections of the masses including parts of the proletariat, undoubtedly represents a backward step on the path towards realisation of the values of the species.

It is also an irrefutable fact that in the abstract, the neo-capitalist system meets the demands of the bourgeoisie better than fascism does. Fascism does not seriously threaten capitalist economic interests (the German bourgeoisie already knew this beforehand), and it channels the anti-capitalist feelings which it entails into the fight against "Jewish" and "non-productive" capital; but at the same time it creates extraordinary political conditions and replaces normal bourgeois everyday life with a situation of constant tension, and the bourgeoisie finds this at least "uncomfortable". The bourgeoisie, in fact, does not welcome the permanent assertion of revolutionary methods even when they are serving a counter-revolutionary purpose. It wants to consolidate. In this context one can justifiably refer to Marx's graphic description of Louis Bonaparte's coup and apply it *mutatis mutandis* to Hitler's seizure of power:

"Finally the high priests of 'religion and order' themselves are kicked from their Pythian tripods, manhandled out of their beds in the darkness of night, put into prison vans, thrown into dungeons or sent into exile; their temple is razed to the ground, their mouths are sealed, their pens broken, their law torn to pieces in the name of religion, of property, of family, of order. Bourgeois fanatics for order are shot down on their balconies by mobs of drunken soldiers, their domestic sanctuaries profaned, their houses bombed for amusement — in the name of property, of family, of religion and of order. Finally the scum of bourgeois society forms the holy phalanx of order, and the hero Crapulinsky installs himself in the Tuileries as the 'saviour of society'."[49]

Trotsky was, of course, wrong to claim that one instrument is as good as another for the bourgeoisie. It is true that before the seizure of power a large part of the German bourgeoisie lived in the belief that as soon as Hitler was appointed chancellor he would turn into an ordinary bourgeois politician. But it was far from being a certainty. Why then, in spite of this, did the German bourgeoisie choose the fascist solution?

There were very few marxists able to actually formulate the question in this way at all. For those who regarded the *form* of bourgeois rule as irrelevant, the question itself was simply immaterial. And for those who maintained that fascism constituted a necessary phase in capitalist development (regardless of whether they saw it as a crisis phenomenon or as the adequate form of that development), it was downright nonsensical.

The "Blum Theses" of Georg Lukács are among the very few exceptions in contemporary marxist literature, in that they resolutely bring up this question. Although the "Blum Theses" comply with the Comintern standpoint by labelling both trends of capitalist development after the war as fascist, they maintain that the "American way", i.e. the democratic form, constitutes the adequate form of this development, and they try to find out what prevented this form from being realised in Europe in spite of the reformist labour bureaucracy's attempts to introduce American-style democracy:

"The labour bureaucracy has very serious economic reasons for taking this stand. Postwar imperialism is forced not to tolerate trade-union struggles of the prewar type in any form, mainly because it must prepare the new world war but also because competition has been affected. It subjects the trade unions to fascism. But this subjection is accomplished in very different ways. One way is Mussolini's: with the help of a counter-revolution based on the petty bourgeoisie and middle peasantry, he destroyed the old trade unions and replaced them with entirely new ones [Lukács, too, saw the essence of fascism of the classic type, i.e. of authentic fascism, as being the annihilation of the trade unions and the destruction of the reformist labour movement — M.V.]. This solution, however, is fraught with dangers for both the bourgeoisie and the labour bureaucracy. It requires a big effort from the bourgeoisie to transform the petty bourgeois counter-revolution into a consolidation on the part of the haute bourgeoisie; and one part of the labour bureaucracy loses its positions in the labour movement (Italian émigrés), while those who accommodate themselves to the fascist system enter an antagonistic relation with the masses of workers. For both the haute bourgeoisie and the labour bureaucracy it is easier and less dangerous to apply the method which has already been introduced in Germany through compulsory arbitration [*staatliche Schlichtungswesen*], and which has partly come into force in Britain too through the Trade Union Act and is destined to be crowned by 'Mond-ism'. Clearly, as far as the proletariat is concerned the class content of both systems is the same. Only the methods differ. And of course this difference in method means that different strata exercise power in the fascist state, or rather that they share this power in different proportions."[50]

If we leave aside for the moment the fact that Lukács also gives the fascist label to those systems in which state intervention reconciles the interests of the bourgeoisie with those of the trade unions, then clearly he regarded the intervention of the state in trade-union struggles as being the fundamental characteristic of capitalist development after the first world war. (And it is quite justifiable to leave aside Lukács's method of nomenclature, since the "Theses" are imbued with the basic idea that as long as the dictatorship of the proletariat is not on the agenda, it is the job of socialists to defend all those forms which can avoid the introduction of a Mussolini-type model.)

There are two possible ways for the state to make its intervention. The first is that the state assumes the function of mediator between the employers and the trade unions (and this obviously implies that the individual capitalist is ready to subordinate his own interests to those of the "state", i.e. to the interests of aggregate capital). The other possibility is that the trade unions can be annihilated or "nationalised" and the whole labour movement liquidated; but this can only be done in a way that is fraught with dangers for the bourgeoisie itself. And so Lukács had already, in 1928, raised the possibility of the alternative which we discussed earlier. It is true that he did not perceive the specific character of the Italian situation, and that his description of Italian fascism applied least of all to Italy. But this is a different question, as is the fact that he exaggerated the difference between the American and British economic situation and the European one, and it was probably caused by the fact that, in concentrating on the Italian example, he identified fascism with economic backwardness.

The "Blum Theses" also raised the question of why one or the other alternative is chosen, and made it clear that in the abstract it was in the interests of both basic classes of society *not* to choose fascism. It is worth quoting Lukács in full on this:

"The close interconnection between monopoly capital and the state had already appeared in the prewar period, and the developments during and after the war intensified it enormously. And the increasing intensification of the class struggle forces the state to create institutional safeguards against it. The disorganisation of the masses, the fact that they are bereft of any influence in state affairs, the abolition of the workers' class struggle by legal means are not new phenomena, but they now occur in new contexts. The reasons are: (a) the political weight and level of the masses today is much higher than it was in earlier stages of development; but as against this, (b) the mass propaganda instruments at the disposal of monopoly capital (the press etc.) are also much more developed, and (c) it is an entirely new phenomenon that these tendencies towards the interconnection between monopoly capital and the state are supported by the official leading section of the working class. Here, too, the USA is the ideal. But in Europe there are funda-

78

mental political and economic differences with the USA. First of all, in the USA (as in the European imperialist states before the war) the upper layer of the working class can be satisfied in material terms because of the huge extent and rapid growth of accumulation, of the export of capital and of super-profits. In Europe there is only a very narrow basis for this development. Secondly, the militant traditions of the European worker are lacking in the USA. And finally, in many European countries the bourgeoisie only became the political ruling class in the postwar period (as in Germany), or it was only then that they received a larger share in political leadership than before (as in Hungary). Therefore, the reconciliation of political democracy on the one hand with an actual lack of influence of the masses and an institutional or forcible suppression of the class struggle on the other, has not reached the American ideal and will not do so. This does not stop the bourgeoisie and the labour bureaucracy from trying to follow the American model. But the foundations of this undertaking must be shakier than in the USA, and therefore no European bourgeoisie will ever entirely dismiss the possibility of the 'classical' (Italian) type of fascism. It will always hold this possibility in reserve and be ready to use it if the class struggle intensifies, if there is open conflict between the masses and the bourgeoisie."[51]

Lukács gave a clear formulation to many of the fundamental conditions for the rise of modern manipulative capitalism: the increased political weight of the working class, the increasing effectiveness of monopoly capital's political propaganda, the incorporation of the leaders of the reformist mass labour organisations into the power structure. He also attempted to enumerate those factors which may induce the bourgeoise, in spite of the fact that fascism has aspects which are unfavourable to it, to use the strength of fascist power to conserve its own rule. According to Lukács, as we have seen, the following factors induced the bourgeoisie to keep the possibility of fascism in store: (a) the fact that the European bourgeoisie (with the exception of Britain) betwen the two world wars was not yet able to satisfy the material needs of the working class; (b) the *militant* traditions of the working class, which were present in every leading European capitalist state besides Britain; and (c) the bourgeoisie's complete lack of experience of political leadership, the complete lack of bourgeois democratic traditions.

It is true that Lukács himself alleged that the bourgeoisie was forced to make use of fascism as an instrument at times of intensifying class struggle. This is a proposition which, as we have already mentioned, does not correspond to the facts: a situation of social crisis does not necessarily mean the intensification of the class struggle. Furthermore, he overestimated the role of economic backwardness in causing a country to turn to fascism (this was because he took the Italian model as a paradigm). But what needs to be emphasised is *the way in which he formulated the question*. In my view the adequate formulation of the question as far as German fascism is concerned runs as follows: what was it that compelled the bourgeoisie to try and find a way out of the 1929-33 crisis by helping fascism to power, even though the extensive phase of capitalist development had already come to an end in Germany? The analysis of the situation which the "Blum Theses" provide contains important parts of my own answer to this question.

XI Why did the German Bourgeoisie Choose Hitler?

First of all, it must be emphasised that this question cannot be solved in terms of one single factor. It cannot be said that the characteristics of the German capitalist economy played no part at all. However, it is beyond doubt a fact that the extensive phase in the development of German capitalism was already over, and that no essential difference existed between the basic characteristics of economic development in Germany and in the other leading capitalist countries (particularly the USA and Britain). And in any case, no such difference would adequately explain the radical difference between the corresponding political solutions in these countries. But this does not mean that we should exclude economic factors from the complex of factors which influenced the choice of a fascist solution.

We need, furthermore, to formulate our question with a greater degree of historical precision. It is quite arbitrary to simply assume that the German bourgeoisie chose the fascist form of rule as a way out of the existing crisis. The question needs to be made more specific. First, could — indeed, did — the leading circles of the German haute bourgeoisie see any other way out of the existing economic, social and political crisis which would not have violated their basic interests? Second, is it actually true that the rise of the nazi dictatorship was brought about by a "decision" of the class which possessed basic economic power, i.e. the bourgeoisie? (We should not forget, in dealing with this problem, that although the large estates in Germany had been capitalised, the landowning aristocracy and the industrial haute bourgeoisie remained two classes with differing interests.) And finally, if fascism gained power in Germany as the result of a decision by the bourgeoisie (not, of course, any single collective decision, but the result of the utmost variety of concrete decisions), did the result correspond to the ruling class's original intentions?

I shall try to answer these questions in the pages which follow. More precisely, relying on the historical data and analyses avail-

81

able to me, I wish to point out the contours of an answer which is based on the assumption (to be proved in detail in the next chapter) that the basic function of German fascism coincided with the basic function of the New Deal: i.e. it created the political conditions for the transition of capitalism from the stage of extensive growth to the stage of intensive development.

From the outbreak of the economic crisis in 1929, the German bourgeoisie was confronted with a dilemma — to put it more precisely, it was at this moment that the "rationality" of the existing political system was explicitly called in question among broad circles of the bourgeoisie. (The rightward shift of the bourgeoisie was to remain characteristic of the régime's brief history.) This explicit doubt took two basic forms. First of all there was a widespread demand for a "firm hand", a need for a political system within which the authority of the executive power would not be continually questioned. For the bourgeoisie, firm political power capable of implementing its decisions means that the state is able to intervene in the functioning of the economy, or at least that it is capable of creating the conditions for its "normal", essentially crisis-free functioning. This bourgeois demand is not specific to Germany. The great economic crisis of 1929 produced similar tendencies all over the world; they were reflected too in Roosevelt's election in 1932. What was specific to the German situation was simply the fact that the bourgeoisie considered itself unable to achieve the creation of a stable political power capable of directing and controlling the economy otherwise than by liquidating the Weimar republic, i.e. the bourgeois democratic system. Secondly, in the eyes of the German bourgeoisie the Weimar democracy appeared to be irrational and inadequate for German conditions because it gave too great a scope for "marxism" — and to them, "marxism" meant not only the communist movement which opposed and attacked the system itself but also the social democrats, who were integrated into the system (though at the political level they had already been forced into opposition). There is no need to explain in detail why in such a serious crisis situation the bourgeoisie disapproved of the legal existence of the communist organisations, which in addition appeared to have much more revolutionary potential than was in fact the case. The reasons for its aversion to the reformist labour movement (which in any case was not, of course, so pronounced) are not so self-evident. But it is only in retrospect that this aversion seems puzzling or irrational. In this particular historical period, the only place where a system functioned that was unequivocally capable of integrating the reformist labour movement completely was Britain. And since British reformism had a different past and present from the continental one, it could hardly have served as a prognostic model for Germany. The neo-capitalist system which was stabilised in all the important Western countries after the second world war was not "planned" by the bourgeoisie, and certainly not by the German one, which was the least self-confident about its ability to "tame" the proletariat. On the other hand, the German bourgeoisie was fully justified in thinking that social democracy had been the principal initiator of the completely unviable Weimar democracy. Social democracy was bent on defending to the last a system which was totally unable to function.

The fact that these two factors lay at the root of the German bourgeoisie's anti-Weimar mood is demonstrated by the January 1932 meeting of the "Economic Union of Employers' Associations", which had as the main topic on its agenda the problem of "Corporational Hierarchisation of the Capitalist Economic Order", with the title of the main report as "How Can Marxism be Liquidated?" The official organisation of the German bourgeoisie considered the corporate state, based on an autarchic planned economy, to be the only way out of the crisis.

The German bourgeoisie consciously strove to replace the Weimar republic with another type of power, with some kind of authoritarian régime. Its economic interests in fact demanded this. For while it may be true that democracy *in general* has not become unviable in the crises of the twentieth century, just as it has not *in general* become incapable of functioning as the political form of neo-capitalist transformation and subsequently of the stabilised neo-capitalist system, the Weimar democracy was in fact quite unsuitable for this role. Yet we can safely say of the Weimar constitution that it was the model constitution of bourgeois democracy. It bore a perfect correspondence to liberal ideas. It tried to guarantee that every particular stratum and group could have its own organisation or party to represent its interests, and that the state's policies would be formed out of the balance created by the continuous confrontation between these interests. This form of liberal democracy has probably never existed in its pure form anywhere. And in Germany, a country where there was no tradition of liberalism at all, it was established at a time when this form had already become out of date. This is not the occasion to analyse the political forms of modern capitalist democracy. But even if we bear only the British or American forms in mind, it is clear that their political mechanisms differ basically from that of Weimar. In addition to the fact that their main political parties are not organs representing the interests of definite and circumscribed social strata (it would be difficult, for example, to assert that the British Labour Party represents the interests of the working class alone), it is also the case that no constant confrontation of interests can or does take place within the framework of these forms. The various interests may clash sharply in the pre-election period: after the elections, however, the group in power is able to carry out its own political line. This was not true of the Weimar republic. Whoever the chancellor was, his activities were constantly obstructed by the Reichstag, and for long periods it was only possible to govern through "presidential cabinets", i.e. governments which did not have the confidence of the Reichstag. In political terms this meant a permanent state of crisis.

At the same time there was another element in the political structure which also contributed to the bankruptcy of the Weimar democracy, and this was its federal character. It was precisely in economic affairs that the Reich government was least able to enforce its will in the Länder.

In these circumstances it was impossible to set up a capitalist system based on state leadership of the economy. The bourgeoisie's basic economic interests demanded the transformation of the political system. But in the years following the outbreak of the economic crisis there was, within the framework of capitalism, no other method of overthrowing the Weimar democracy than by transferring power to the nazis. The bourgeoisie clearly saw that in Germany it would be impossible to create a strong capitalist state capable of directing the economy with social democratic help. The latter struck rigidly to the Weimar framework, which was obsolete and had never really been viable. And *in spite of* the social democrats, the Weimar régime could only be overthrown with the help of the nazis. In 1928 the situation was not yet clearcut; there were still hopes of stabilisation. But by 1930 it was unequivocal.

From 1930 onwards Germany had a presidential dictatorship relying first on the centre and then primarily on a rightist alliance between the bourgeoisie and the landowners. But this could not generate stability, for in the absence of a strong army the overthrow of the Weimar régime by a putsch and the restitution of the monarchy allied with the two ruling classes was impossible. In addition to this, the economic measures of Brüning's conservative "centre government" failed to get over the crisis or pave the way towards a system of state intervention. Quite the contrary. The successful results of the Roosevelt presidency's economic policy in its first few months and of the Schacht policy after Hitler's rise to power showed that the economic crisis could only be solved by inflationary measures providing open state subsidies to the economy, and not by deflationary austerity measures. And a majority capable of changing the Weimar constitution could not be brought about by "democratic" (i.e. constitutional) means: the constitution could be amended only by a two-thirds majority, and the right — including the nazis — did not possess the required number of seats even after the March 1933 elections.

The first of the two questions which I posed at the beginning of this chapter may therefore be answered in the negative. It is an irrefutable fact that the German bourgeoisie had a basic interest in liquidating the Weimar democracy, and that this could only be carried out with the help of the nazis. It cannot be denied, either, that because of this the German bourgeoisie chose this way out more or less consciously, "voluntarily": our answer to the second question, then, is in the affirmative. Of course, it is not in the least true that everything which happened afterwards during the course of nazi rule corresponded to the German bourgeoisie's intentions. For once the bourgeoisie had allowed Hitler to gain power, it no longer had any choice.

The factors we have already dealt with by no means exhaust the problem. Why did the national socialist movement evolve with such a sweeping force in the crisis years, and why did it become such a determining factor in German political life that the bourgeoisie could only solve its problems by supporting this movement?

The question cannot be dismissed by saying simply that the

German bourgeoisie helped fascism to power so as to solve its own problems and extricate itself from the economic and political crisis. There is no doubt that the German bourgeoisie did help Hitler, in two ways. First of all, there were influential capitalist circles (though by no means all the leading bourgeois power groups) who gave the movement financial support. And secondly, they never took an energetic stand against the apparatus of nazi violence; at the same time they took strict steps against the "unconstitutional acts" of the communists, though these were generally much less significant or violent. But the importance of these factors is often exaggerated, and they do not answer the question. If the bourgeoisie was so powerful that it was able to take a tiny movement (in 1928 the nazis still only had eight hundred thousand voters!) and turn it into the largest party in the country, then why did it not use its power to bring about a form of rule that corresponded to its own "tastes" and objectives? The masses who eventually followed the nazis (on the eve of power they numbered thirteen million) were not created by the bourgeoisie, who in fact voted for the centre and the non-nazi right; there were considerable sectors of the German population who were not big capitalists and who nevertheless wanted the nazi solution.

In the previous section I tried to show that nazi ideology expressly reflected the aspirations of the middle classes and that these layers felt drawn to the nazi organisational form too. It is a historical fact that a very large number of nazi voters came from the ranks of the middle classes. There were some from the towns, but primarily it was the village petty bourgeoisie (peasants, white-collar employees and officials) who voted for the nazis. So if it could be proved that the 1929 crisis affected the middle classes first of all, and that they bore a greater burden in Germany than in the other countries affected by the crisis, then we would have a complete explanation for the advance of nazism. But unfortunately this is only partly true.

It is true to the extent that there was a similar primary determinant in the development of German fascism as there was in Italian. The powerful reformist mass organisations of the German working class, which participated in political power too, were able to secure relatively good working-class living conditions (mainly for those still employed, and especially the older organised workers among them), even during the crisis period. They were able to gain some relief for the unemployed. The bourgeoisie was forced to place the burden of the welfare measures on the middle classes. It was true, therefore, that during the crisis period the power of the reformist labour movement did in fact threaten the middle classes. (We should also not forget the fact that in the USA these measures were only introduced later, during the recovery period.) The power of the reformist labour movement also explains why no radicalisation of the working class took place in Germany during the crisis, as it did in France or the USA. The organised workers stuck to the status quo, which undoubtedly brought them some advantages. At the same time, only a small part of the unorganised and unemployed workers moved to the left. This can be explained partly by the social origin of this section, which we have already mentioned in the preceding chapter, and partly by the rootlessness of the German communists' policies: now (obviously hopeless) revolutionary moves, now the adoption of the right's own slogans, now an insistence on "democracy" — without any concrete indication of a way out.

In this sense, therefore, the crisis indeed fell heavier on the middle classes than on the proletariat, and hurt them more in Germany than in the other capitalist countries. But this does not explain everything. There were other factors which contributed to the radicalisation of the middle classes.

The peasants' situation was completely hopeless. The world crisis did not, of course, only afflict the German peasant; the American farmers and the French peasants were in just as difficult a situation. But the German peasants felt themselves threatened by the large estates too. This was in spite of the fact that they were traditionally rightist, and remained so partly because no one among the socialists paid any attention to their problems. Even though the nazis did not say a word about democratic land reform, nevertheless the village petty bourgeoisie, the peasantry which found itself in a more and more hopeless situation, played a fundamental role in the sudden growth of the national socialist movement, and especially in the rapid extension of its vote. Hitler exploited the fact that not a single political movement or party had paid any attention to this not inconsiderable sector of the population. So he took up their interests. The nazi programme and the faction fights inside the nazi party indicate clearly how Hitler consciously strove to win mass support for his party among the peasants. His break with the Strasser brothers shows this well. In accordance with the party's actual name, they tried to broaden the mass basis of the movement beyond the urban petty bourgeoisie and lumpen elements, primarily by recruiting from the ranks of the working class. Hitler knew that although his nationalistic programme might win over a small number of embittered and backward workers from the communists (and this actually did happen — by 1933 he had won about a million voters away from the left), he could not capture really broad sections of the working class; and in fact he did not reach the social democratic workers at all. His rapprochement with Walter Darré, the author of the "Blood and Soil" programme, which took place just after his break with Otto Strasser, showed clearly how resolute his intention was to gain the peasants' support against the workers. In the unanimous opinion of the historians, Darré's agrarian programme was the most reasoned (and, in most respects, the least executed) part of the nazi programme.

The execution of the programme was based on the same aggressive expansionism which characterised all nazi ideology. If the basic problems of the peasantry were to be solved in such a way as to leave the large estates intact, then there could be no further fragmentation of peasant smallholdings (this was prevented by the *Erbhofgesetz,* the law on land inheritance), and peasant sons driven off their fathers' lands had to be promised some *Lebensraum,* i.e. good quality land belonging to Slavs. It was no accident that the SS was made up mainly of young peasants.

The German bourgeoisie could only have retained its political power (i.e. it could only have found a way out of the crisis without relying on the nazis) by solving the problems of the village petty bourgeoisie, the peasantry. But there were only two ways of doing this: either by the radical, democratic transformation of agrarian conditions (and the German bourgeoisie, whose attitudes towards the old ruling classes were servile and impotent, was incapable of this), or by territorial expansion. The German bourgeoisie was not up to this latter task either. It was not confident enough of its position to think seriously of any revision of the Versailles treaty, not to mention the fact that it would have been hopeless to try and drive the social democratic masses of workers directly into a new war.

There was, however, another factor to explain the radicalisation of the middle classes: the lost war, and the consequences of the unjust peace treaty which had followed. This had had a direct effect on the position of the German middle classes: the "unemployment" of army officers, the economic crisis and inflation which ruined a considerable part of the petty bourgeosie (this crisis was understandably more serious in Germany than in the other capitalist countries), etc. But its direct effects had an even greater importance. From 1929 onwards, after five years of prosperity, the middle classes once again felt their situation becoming hopeless, and they turned with anger and bitterness against the Weimar democracy; and it was the forces behind Weimar that they held primarily responsible for defeat in the war (the *Dolchstoss* or "stab in the back" theory) and for making it possible for the Western powers to enforce the Versailles treaty on Germany.

These circumstances turned large sectors of the population against the Weimar republic. This was true even during the revolutionary period of 1919-20: in 1919 the number of right-wing voters was only four and a half million, but by 1920 they already numbered ten million. But it was not inevitable that they should turn to the nazis. And it was precisely here that the national *socialism* of the nazis played a role. These sectors of the population, as opposed to the ruling classes, were against the Weimar republic not because of their antagonism towards socialism in principle, but because of their nationalist mentality. As soon as they saw a strong and influential party promising *both* the improvement of their social position *and* the "rise" of the German nation, they immediately joined it.

As we can see, there were many factors that played into the nazis' hands. Hitler proved to be a brilliant tactician. He knew how to exploit all the moments which might carry him forward to the seizure of power, cleverly combining revolutionary methods with parliamentary tactics, anti-capitalist slogans with willingness to negotiate with the capitalists, and so on.

In the fourth year of the crisis there was only one force capable of doing away with the existing, non-viable system for good. This was the nazis, and there was no other way out for the bourgeoisie than to hand political power over to them. The bourgeoisie thus contributed to the birth of a system which imposed much harsher conditions on the average citizen than the prewar régime did. It could not have foreseen the true nature of the system at the moment when it handed over power. But the bourgeoisie's hopes proved, in a historical perspective, not to be entirely unjustified. Out of the universal conflagration unleashed by the war, the nazi system created a Germany in which all the elements of the normal functioning of *modern* capitalism were now present.

THE POWER AND RULE OF THE FASCIST SYSTEM

XII Fascism and Bonapartism

In two European countries the fascist movement achieved its goal. The party gained power, and the dictatorship was established. In the two countries different factors motivated (or forced) the ruling bourgeoisie into handing political power over to the fascists. In accordance with their different origins, the two systems fulfilled different economic functions. But their structure — not only their political structure but their social structure too — can be regarded as essentially identical. Which class (stratum) or classes actually benefited from the fascist régime? I am in agreement with Horkheimer when he says that "whoever does not like speaking about 'capitalism' would have kept quiet about fascism too".[52] In fact, fascism in no way restricted the bourgeoisie's economic power within the factory. It did not thwart their economic interests and even helped them obtain increased satisfaction. After the downfall of the fascist régime in both countries, the fact that it had existed at all brought about a new régime which guaranteed the political rule of the haute bourgeoisie. In many respects, the fascist régime determined the nature of the new one. But this does not contradict my assertion that in the fascist system the bourgeoisie does not itself exercise political power, and that in fact it lacks a voice in the decisions of those who are ruling politically. Consequently, our understanding of the essence of fascism is helped very little by the statement that fascism is the rule of finance capital. This is only true in the sense that fascism primarily served and satisfied the interests of the haute bourgeoisie, and it carries very little conviction if it is left unexplained. This characterisation of fascism is not confined to marxists alone, and can be reached from a non-marxist position too. For example, Hermann Heller writes that "all in all, fascism cannot be considered a new form of state, it is nothing but the form of dictatorship adequate to capitalist society".[53]

But on the other hand, we obviously cannot confine ourselves simply to a sociological description of the fascist power "élite", or to a debate about which stratum exercises power in fascism

93

and how it does so. We cannot simply take it for granted that fascism is evidently one of the forms of rule of the capitalist system. This is why I find Iring Fetscher's definition unsatisfactory:

"In its ideo-typical pure form, fascism is the rule of a radical minority, a minority which consists in essence of militarised and déclassé petty bourgeois, lumpenproletarian and half-educated elements, which exploits the propertied classes' fear of bolshevism and socialisation as well as the conservatives' aversion to the parliamentary system, in order to induce them to accept the seizure of power by this minority. Its objective is the destruction of political and social pluralism and the realisation of the unrestricted rule of a new 'élite', an élite which utilises any conceivable means in order to secure and extend its power, and which justifies this rule by a historical myth of a racial or some other kind."[54]

There is not much in Fetscher's description that one can object to. Everything he says is true. But since he does not raise the question of the real connections between fascism and the economic structure (although he never actually denies that fascism leaves property relations intact), he fails to give a satisfactory explanation — just as the Comintern definition (which simply restated that fascism maintains the haute bourgeoisie's economic power unbroken) failed.

The most adequate approach to the analysis of fascist dictatorship is, I think, to approach it on the basis of Marx's analysis of bonapartism in *The Eighteenth Brumaire of Louis Bonaparte*. As we have already seen, August Thalheimer made a categorical attempt to do this. He follows Marx's analysis of the bonapartist system step by step, in order to prove that fascism corresponds in every respect with the notion of bonapartist dictatorship. He writes:

"The common denominator [of bonapartism and fascism] is the open dictatorship of capital. Its form of appearance is characterised by the fact that the executive power becomes independent, that the political power of the bourgeoisie is destroyed and all the other social classes become politically subordinated to the executive power. But its social or class content is determined by the rule of the bourgeoisie and of the private proprietors in general over the working class and over all the other strata exploited by capital."[55]

Trotsky argued against Thalheimer and the German communist opposition, saying that only the period just preceding the fascist seizure of power (the Brüning and Papen governments) were bonapartist. The debate between Thalheimer and Trotsky appears to have been in many ways a mere scholastic exercise; we cannot substitute analogies for the real analysis of a historical phenomenon, even if analogies can help in elucidating certain problems. It can be demonstrated that both the period of the Brüning and Papen governments and the fascist dictatorship itself corresponded in various ways with bonapartism. But would it constitute a theoretical advance if we could actually show that one of them "fulfilled" Marx's definition better than the other? Is there any sense at all in trying to determine whether fascism is a bonapartist régime or not?

From a historical perspective it may indeed seem to be a piece of senseless hair-splitting to debate the bonapartist nature of fascism. Nevertheless, I do not agree with those who think that the problem itself is a senseless one, as for example Angelo Tasca did when he said that "fascism is a postwar phenomenon, and every attempt to define it with the help of historically 'antecedent' parallels, e.g. by analogy with bonapartism, remains unproductive and may be misleading".[56] It is true that there are many respects in which fascism cannot be compared to any previous historical phenomenon. Perhaps it is more than just our moral sense that revolts against mentioning Hitler's horrors and the rule of Louis Bonaparte, let alone Napoleon, in the same breath. But even if it could be proved that the two historical phenomena had nothing essentially in common, I would still consider it undeniably valuable that some marxists should have made the analogy between bonapartism and fascist dictatorship or the forms of rule which immediately led up to it. For by the very act of proposing this analogy, which in itself can never supply the key to understanding of a concrete historical phenomenon, they are accomplishing a theoretical task: they are reviving one of Marx's most brilliant analyses, the outstanding example of the analysis of political rule, political structure and economic relations as a complex.

Marx's analysis reminds our contemporaries that the theoretical examination of the actual state and characteristics of a régime must be based on an analysis of the inter-relations among all the classes and strata involved in it. Marx made a clearcut distinction between those who actually hold the reins of political rule and the classes and strata that exercise economic power. His analysis of bonapartism clearly demonstrates that the tasks of politico-sociological analysis are not exhausted simply by the examination of property relations, and that the property relations in themselves do not determine the political structure of the system. *The Eighteenth Brumaire* proved to be a fertile point of departure (quite independently of whether or not it proves that fascism meets all the basic characteristics of bonapartism), because it drew attention to something which marxist theory as received by both social democracy and stalinism denies. This is the fact that it is possible (and was actually the case at points in history before fascism) for a political system to exist in which political rule is not exercised by the fundamental class in the given social formation, i.e. not by the class which possesses the decisive means of production. Regardless of whether fascism is bonapartism or not, we are clearly not compelled to make a theoretically untenable choice between two false alternatives: either, by looking at the unbroken and even reinforced power of monopoly capital under fascism, to assert that the fascist system was built directly on the rule of monopoly capital, or, by examining the social origins of the stratum in power and its relation to the means of production, to deny the increased economic power of monopoly capital.

One of the most important messages of *The Eighteenth Brumaire* is that the bourgeoisie, as the leading social class, has its own very important specific feature which distinguishes it from the ruling classes of all preceding societies: it does not insist on the exercise of political rule under all circumstances. In bourgeois society, the individual has been severed from the umbilical cord of the community. His place in "civil society", in the egoistic world of economic interests, does not determine his role in the ideal sphere of the political state. In all preceding, "naturally given" societies, where "civil society" and "political state" were not yet separate, those who held economic power always operated as the political leaders of society, directly and (as a result of their economic position) automatically. In bourgeois society this is no longer true. The bourgeois is a bourgeois as long, but only as long, as he possesses capital, and if he does possess it he can satisfy his particular needs more or less unrestrictedly, without having to be a member of the stratum which rules the society and determines the political activity of the ideal community. For this very reason, the capitalist has little inclination to abandon his private activities and act politically, and even less to subordinate his private (i.e. bourgeois) existence to his public, political (i.e. citizen's) existence: "the ordinary bourgeois [is] always inclined to sacrifice the general interest of his class for this or that private motive".[57] If possible, he attends to his business and does not get involved in politics. And what is true of the individual bourgeois is essentially true also of his class. In the everyday life of civil society, the bourgeoisie does not act as a class. The class interest only comes to the fore (as that of the "community", to which the individual bourgeois must subordinate his egoistic interests) at moments when the class is threatened. It follows from the structure and the functional mechanisms of this society, and above all from the separation between "civil society" and "political state", that the same holds true *mutatis mutandis* for the other classes in it too.

As long as the rule of another class prevented the bourgeoisie from freely asserting its own egoistic material interests, it was of course forced to appear as an independent political force. Until the bourgeoisie succeeded in getting rid of the feudal ruling class (as happened in France), or in forcing it into a position where it could not, in spite of its maintenance of political rule, frustrate the bourgeoisie from asserting its own material interests (as happened in Britain), it reluctantly accepted the necessity for political struggle and for the political form of existence. But as soon as the bourgeoisie could develop its material power without restrictions, political activity became a burden to it and simply obstructed its attempts to realise the opportunities it had fought so hard for. Consequently, it was sometimes prepared to abandon politics to a class or stratum which was ready to exercise it.

The first and purest historical form of this example was to be observed in France. This was no accident. Because of the resistance which it met, the French bourgeoisie fought the purest and most classical form of struggle against the feudal class. This meant that, as a class possessing real economic power, it remained essentially alone. The British bourgeoisie had already made a compromise, and only the subsequent behaviour of the French bourgeoisie made it clear that as a result of this compromise the British bourgeoisie had escaped lightly. It was only the French bourgeoisie which, by carrying its struggle through to full political victory, "proved that the struggle to maintain its *public* interests, its own class *interests*, its *political power*, only troubled and upset it as a disturbance of private business".[58]

In *The Eighteenth Brumaire* Marx also demonstrated that it was not only burdensome but often dangerous for the bourgeoisie to maintain its rule in pure form. The bourgeoisie could only fight feudalism if it presented its own particular interests as the general interest (and believed them to be so). But as soon as it brought about its own rule in pure form, the ideological nature of its ideals was revealed:

> "Instinct taught them that the republic indeed perfects their political rule, but at the same time undermines its social foundation, since they must now confront the subjugated classes and contend against them without intermediation. . . . It was a feeling of weakness that caused them to recoil from the pure conditions of their own class rule, and to sigh for the less complete, less developed and consequently less dangerous forms of this rule."[59]

The question of whether or not the bourgeoisie renounces its own political rule — and if so, in what form — always depends on the concrete, historically given class relations of the country concerned. Bonapartist dictatorship is only one (extreme) form of solution. But it is a form in which the bourgeoisie renounces its *political* power alone, for the sake of maintaining its *social* power:

> "The bourgeoisie confess that their own interest dictates that they should be rescued from the danger of governing in their own name; that in order to restore tranquillity in the land, the bourgeois parliament must first of all be given its quietus; that in order to preserve its social power inviolate, its political power must be broken; that the private bourgeois can only continue to exploit the other classes and to enjoy undisturbed property, family, religion and order on condition that their class be condemned along with the other classes to a like political nullity; that in order to save its purse it must abandon the crown; and that the sword which is to safe-

guard it must be hung over its own head as a sword of Damocles."[60]

When Engels wrote to Marx in 1866 that "bonapartism is after all the real religion of the modern bourgeoisie",[61] he was already using the notion of bonapartism in a generalised sense. His choice of words expresses precisely the idea that the bourgeoisie is seldom able to rule alone. Depending on the historical conditions, the bourgeoisie often shares the exercise of political rule with other strata or classes (for example the old feudal ruling strata) or leaves it entirely to them, as long as it has previously made sure that the latter cannot restrict the growth of its economic power. (In many cases the bourgeoisie did not even make an attempt to seize power, as was the case in Bismarck's Germany.) Moreover, we can nowadays see that the bourgeoisie may even accept circumstances where political leadership is in the hands of proletarian parties (social democratic governments). I have already indicated what kind of conditions enable it to acquiesce in this kind of situation: there must be separation between civil society and the political state, so that even in "normal" circumstances political power is not exercised directly by the bourgeoisie but by an "independent" apparatus, which in these "normal" circumstances depends directly on the bourgeoisie. It is relatively rare for the bourgeoisie to transfer political power to a genuinely independent apparatus — that is, to a socially separate stratum which can only secure a source of livelihood by taking over executive power. This happens if a stratum exists which has somehow been driven out by "civil society" but which, because of its origins or the economic situation of the country, cannot be reintegrated at a lower level. Louis Bonaparte's Tenth of December Society was of this nature. The existence of the Society made Louis Bonaparte a political factor in France, although he did not mean or represent anything at all in French "civil society":

"The Tenth of December Society belonged to him, it was *his* work, his very own idea. Whatever else he appropriates is put into his hands by force of circumstances; whatever else he does the circumstances do for him, or he is content to copy from the deeds of others. . . . The Tenth of December Society was thus to remain the private army of Bonaparte, until he succeeded in transforming the public army into a Tenth of December Society."[62]

99

This kind of organisation and its leader, separated as they are from bourgeois existence, have tremendous advantages over the ordinary bourgeois and also over the "ordinary" bourgeois politician, who clearly stands in a dependent relation to the bourgeoisie itself. They have the advantage over all those who, precisely because of their functions in bourgeois life, have to preserve their "credit". "Because [Bonaparte] was a bohemian, a princely lumpenproletarian, he had the advantage over any rascally bourgeois in that he could conduct the struggle meanly."[63]

Precisely because the only way for this stratum to acquire any social function at all is to take over executive power, it regards the maintenance of this power as a question of livelihood, a question of its own existence; for this very reason, it must also acquire guarantees against the bourgeoisie, just in case the bourgeoisie should no longer need it. In order to maintain his rule, the "head" of society, Bonaparte, must grant huge advantages to his own stratum: "alongside the actual classes of society, he is forced to create an artificial caste, for which the maintenance of his régime becomes a bread-and-butter question".[64] The stratum which rules politically must defend itself from the bourgeoisie:

"As the executive authority which has made itself an independent power, Bonaparte feels it to be his mission to safeguard 'bourgeois order'. But the strength of this bourgeois order lies in the middle class and issues decrees in this sense. Nevertheless, he is somebody solely due to the fact that he has broken the political power of this middle class and daily breaks it anew. Consequently, he looks on himself as the adversary of the political and literary power of the middle class. But by protecting its material power, he generates its political power anew. The cause must accordingly be kept alive; but the effect, where it manifests itself, must be done away with. But this cannot pass off without slight confusions of cause and effect, since in their interaction both lose their distinguishing features. New decrees, that obliterate the borderline. As against the bourgeoisie, Bonaparte looks on himself, at the same time, as the representative of the peasants and of the people in general, who wants to make the lower classes of the people happy within the framework of bourgeois society. New decrees, that cheat the 'true socialists of their statecraft in advance. But above all, Bonaparte looks on himself as the chief of the Tenth of December Society, as the representative of the lumpenproletariat to which he himself, his entourage, his government and his army belong, and whose prime consideration is to benefit itself and draw California lottery prizes from the state treasury. And he vindicates his position as chief of the Tenth of December Society with decrees, without decrees, and despite decrees."[65]

According to Marx's analysis, the essential feature of bonapartism is the independence of executive power exercised by a stratum which has no other function in "civil society", and which is prepared if necessary to act against any class of society in the name of any other class. Nevertheless, I do not think it possible to read into his analysis the conclusion that in bourgeois society, state power and the state machinery are gradually emancipated from society. Marx analysed the gradual growth of bureaucracy from the period of absolute monarchy to the period of the parliamentary republic, and his conclusion was:

"Under the absolute monarchy, during the first revolution, and under Napoleon, bureaucracy was only the means of preparing the class rule of the bourgeoisie. Under the Restoration, under Louis Philippe and under the parliamentary republic, it was the instrument of the ruling class, however much it strove for power of its own. Only under the second Bonaparte does the state *seem* [my italics — M.V.] to have made itself completely independent."[66]

So this was mere appearance, for Bonaparte in fact represented a certain class: "the state power is not suspended in mid-air. Bonaparte represents a class, and the most numerous class of French society at that, the *small peasants*".[67] This class, however, can only partly be described as a class, inasmuch as its members' conditions of existence "derive their mode of life, their interests and their culture from those of the other classes and put them in hostile contrast to the latter".[68] But on the other hand, it is not and cannot be a class, inasmuch as "the identity of their interests begets no unity, no national union and no political organisation".[69] So the executive power can make itself independent only by virtue of the fact that it is held by a quasi-class unable to represent itself.

Therefore the theory[70] that Marx, repudiating the standpoint

101

of *The Communist Manifesto*, gradually came to see the developmental trend of bourgeois society as pointing towards the growth of independence of the executive power, has no foundation in *The Eighteenth Brumaire*. It is factually false, since no such trend can actually be observed in the history of capitalism. It appears only in those periods (and *The Eighteenth Brumaire* points this out) when on the one hand the exercise of political rule has for some reason become inconvenient or even dangerous for the bourgeoisie, and on the other hand a stratum exists which has no function in "civil society" and can only acquire a role through the exercise of executive power. But according to Marx, this power represents the interests of some class in bourgeois society even then. Marx also showed why the bourgeoisie consented to having its free movement and the free exercise of its everyday life restricted by an executive power of this kind, with its tendency to "become independent". The bourgeois tolerates these restrictions because otherwise he would only have the proletariat to rely on in fighting this mob:

> "Instead of letting itself be intimidated by the executive power with the prospect of fresh disturbances, it ought rather to have allowed the class struggle a little elbow-room, so as to keep the executive power dependent on it. But it did not feel equal to the task of playing with fire."[71]

The real lesson of *The Eighteenth Brumaire*, therefore, is not that it points to some alleged tendency of the executive power to become independent. It lies in its recognition that there are cases where the bourgeoisie willingly surrenders the direct exercise of political power to other strata, and sometimes even to those which assert only the egoistic and material interests of the bourgeoisie, while considerably curtailing its civic rights. Naturally, when the bourgeoisie is in power it does its best to avoid this separation from the executive power.

All this amply shows that Marx's analysis of bonapartism is well suited, down to its details, to serve as the point of departure for an analysis of fascist dictatorship. We may also conclude that Thalheimer was certainly right in his debate with Trotsky: for even if it is true that the Brüning and Papen governments existed by exploiting a class equilibrium which at that given moment seemed impossible to budge, nevertheless it was not true that, while these governments were ruling with the help of presidential decrees, executive power rested on a Hitlerite "Tenth of December Society". It rested on the traditional ruling strata and on the constitutional organs of coercion. But as I have already said, I think it would be unproductive to analyse this debate, and that therefore it is unnecessary to assess Thalheimer's "bonapartist" model of fascism in detail. Griepenburg and Tjaden[72] are right when they say that the basic shortcoming of Thalheimer's theory is its rigidity. He works with predetermined constants, and as a result he uses Marx's analysis of bonapartism to describe fascism as a phenomenon (he looks for identities and differences), rather than using it as a starting-point for the exploration, with Marx's help, of the *historically specific* aspects of fascism. This accounts for the somewhat unhistorical nature of his analysis:

> "In this model of politico-social evolution, both the class-constituting, socio-economic antagonism and the separation between economic reproduction and state power are in principle postulated as constants, as permanently present moments of bourgeois society, while the variables consist in the political dispositions of the social classes and strata. These latter determine the change in the 'totality of class relations' and discontinuously, in the specific structure and specific functions of state power."[73]

The determinants of fascism are not correlated to the basic factors of the social totality. The result is that we get an answer to the question, what is fascism? but no answer to the question, at which stage in capitalist development does the real danger of fascism, as the modern variety of bonapartism, concretely arise? If the opposition between economic reproduction and state power is a permanent feature of bourgeois society, then fascism may arise at any time, not simply as the product of specific historical conditions. (It needs to be stressed, however, that Thalheimer came up with his theory under the immediate threat of fascism, and this explains why he emphasised the nature of fascism rather than its historical origins and possibilities.) Thalheimer's restricted viewpoint also prevents him from bringing out one of the most fundamental features of fascist bonapartism: the fact that the fascist leaders did not only have to satisfy the demands of their own private army (which was much larger than Bonaparte's) but had to make sure of much wider mass support too.

Nevertheless there are several ways in which Thalheimer's

103

bonapartist-based analytic model of fascism is justified. The fascist seizure of power meant that the bourgeoisie parted with direct political rule and handed it over to a stratum which had been driven out of the direct reproduction of bourgeois society. The fascist masses, as I have already mentioned, consisted primarily of the middle classes, who felt existentially threatened; the fascist "élite" was recruited from strata without any stable existence.[75] Furthermore, with fascism the executive power achieved an entirely independent role and entirely determined its own policies. These two interrelated aspects make it quite justified to consider fascism a form of bonapartism. Anyone who denies that these two features did in fact characterise fascist rule is simply not worth arguing with. To deny that Hitler and Mussolini exercised their rule by annihilating even the traditional bourgeois parties and ignoring all the legal limitations is to disregard the facts of history completely.

The question is not even whether the broad circles of the bourgeoisie were able to influence political life under fascism, or whether they had any institutional safeguards for the representation of their interests. The answer is clearly in the negative. The real question is whether the *leading personalities* in the important bourgeois circles were capable of directing the fascist régime's policies or at least of influencing them, and to what extent. The answer to this question is by no means so definite, although we shall see later that it is equally a simplification, even a falsification of the actual state of affairs to say that monopoly capital directly dictated the fascist Führer's policies, so to speak, or that Mussolini and Hitler were only puppets in the hands of the haute bourgeoisie which possessed economic power. But even if we come to the conclusion that the leading bourgeois circles were incapable of concretely determining the policies of the fascist régime, we would still not be denying that the fascist régime's policies in the last resort *served the interests* of the leading bourgeoisie circles — if need be, even against the bourgeoisie itself.

XIII   The Italian Dictatorship

It was certainly in the interest of the Italian bourgeoisie to sacrifice their political and civic rights to their economic interests.
After this, no more sacrifices were demanded of them. If Mussolini had not bound his fate to Hitler's absolutely, none of his
political objectives would have endangered the bourgeoisie's particular interests in any way whatsoever. The liquidation of the
labour movement removed the obstacles from the path of capital
accumulation. Industrial development was launched. As a result,
the economy was able to provide employment for those strata
which had previously been driven out of production, and the
sources of mass dissatisfaction were thus considerably reduced.
The economic take-off even made a slow rise in the workers' living
standards possible.

The internal tensions in the Italian fascist dictatorship were
the result of Mussolini's inability to satisfy the demands of the
fascist movement itself, or to maintain a "permanent counter-
revolution". Italian fascism was a simple negation. It had no
concrete *political* objectives (in Germany this permanent task
existed: it was the "solution" of the Jewish question and the
preparation and launching of an aggressive war). Up to the point
when it gained power, Italian fascism's aim was power itself. But
once it had gained power, it became obvious that the movement
lacked any further political objectives and that the exercise of
executive power could guarantee a living for only a small minority
of the movement. Mussolini's own version of the "Tenth of
December Society" was too extended for the majority of its
members to become direct participants in the execution of power.
Once Mussolini had consolidated his power he attempted to cut
the movement down as much as possible. But by doing this he
created a situation where the bourgeoisie could dismiss the fascist
clique any time it felt this to be in its own interest.

Almost certainly this was what induced Mussolini to let himself in for the Abyssinian adventure, which proved to be a turning-point in the history of Italian fascism. On the one hand the

war itself was a "national act" and thereby satisfied the demands of the fascist movement temporarily. On the other hand, however, it caused a confrontation between Italy and her Western allies and led her into almost complete isolation. Italy could only break out of this isolation by improving her relationship with Germany and by a complete reorientation of foreign policy. But with this, Mussolini in a certain sense did away with the "self-sufficiency" and independence of Italian fascism: not because he artificially maintained the external tension in order to hold the movement together (the leaders of German fascism did the same thing), but because in Italy the creation of this artificial tension served no economic function whatsoever. (Since Italian industrial development was still in its extensive phase at this period, working-class living standards did not have to give way to the war industry.) In fact it actually served foreign interests. Because of the alliance with Hitler, Italian fascism lost its "national" character, and this made possible the development of a broad anti-fascist movement into a *national resistance*. This was the main reason why the Italian people, as opposed to the Germans, turned against fascism on a massive scale, and why the anti-fascist struggle had a much larger range in Italy than in any other country allied to Hitler. And in the end, when the country was threatened from outside, the Italian ruling classes succeeded in dismissing the fascist leadership.

For this reason, I would maintain that the fate of Italian fascism, the "rise and fall" of the régime, was of a "non-classical" nature. If our description of the fascist mass movement in Chapter III is true, i.e. if it (apparently) removes the contradiction of particular interests within the nation by counterposing the "nation" as a particular entity against all other nations as particularities, then fascism cannot follow its "classical" path to the end, but must persist with the defence of particular national interests. This same persistent attitude must also at the same time be used to create tensions, which keep the movement in permanent existence; and if the country is not really threatened from the outside by other powers, this presupposes continual, aggressively expansionist policies. If, however, this aggressiveness obviously serves not one's own particular interests but those of another nation, as was true of Italy, then the failure of the policy will produce the exact opposite of its desired effect: far from

106

keeping the movement in existence, it will completely annihilate it. Before its alliance with nazi Germany, Italian fascism faced two alternatives. Either it could renounce all its aggressive claims, thus necessarily changing into an ordinary dictatorship without any broader mass support, relying basically on the regular military organisations and being *directly* dependent on the classes which possessed economic power (in which case the fate of Mussolini and his leading clique would have been placed directly in the hands of the bourgeoisie); or it could subordinate its aggressive policies to foreign interests. It had no other choice.

Clearly, then, our description of Italian fascism as a "non-classical" type is based not only on the fact that certain specific and unique economic factors (which were no longer characteristic of developed capitalism) played a part in its birth, but also on considerations applicable to its whole history (although these were naturally determined to a large extent by the economic factors). It may be argued on methodological grounds that such a view involves a quite arbitrary handling of the historical material. It would mean using the criterion of an abstract "ideal type" of fascism to describe and assess the concrete historical régimes and put them into "classical" or "non-classical" categories. Without going into any lengthy methodological arguments, I shall simply refer to Marx, who set the example. When he spoke about economic development he only mentioned Britain, and when he spoke about political development he only mentioned France. These constituted the respective classic types of capitalist development.

I shall, however, briefly indicate why this procedure is not an arbitrary one. Our starting-point was the common characteristic of both dictatorships: they were both born in the form of broad mass movements, and they both seized power with the support of these movements. If they insist on preserving their power without losing their mass support, they must somehow satisfy the demands and aspirations which the movement has sprung from. If the régime no longer strives for this aim, or if for some reason it is unable to realise it in practice, then it necessarily loses its original character. The *development* of Italian fascism is not classical. But the reason for this is not that it fails to correspond with our arbitrary preconceptions, but that it fails to fulfil the internal conditions of survival of the given social system. The German development, on the other hand, can be considered classical because it enabled the essential internal requirements of the system to be satisfied, and therefore made room for the full evolution of its inner "possibilities".

XIV The German Dictatorship

Those who have investigated the relationship between the nazi régime or movement and the German haute bourgeoisie have usually set out from an analysis of the contacts which the Nazi Party's leaders made with the representatives of monopoly capital in the period before the seizure of power. Those who want to show the close connection between fascism and the interests of monopoly capitalism look for the open or secret channels through which the latter's financial support flowed to the Nazi Party. Those who want to prove the opposite take great pains to show that it was only a narrow bourgeois circle — not even the most important one — which supported Hitler, while the majority was at least neutral. Hundreds of volumes have been written on the subject. But while the presentation of this empirical evidence and counter-evidence helps to determine the concrete responsibility of certain bourgeois circles and personalities, it is in principle an inadequate way of dealing with the theoretical problems. We might even be able to prove that the German haute bourgeoisie supported the fascists unreservedly to a man, before, during and after the seizure of power: but we still would not have proved that fascism served the interests of that class. We would merely have proved that this class was responsible for the birth, ascendancy and conservation of the fascist movement and its power. This, of course, as far as the class rather than the specific personalities are concerned, does not need any concrete proof. Even if none of the class's members had supported Hitler personally it would still be responsible for fascism, since it had been and remained the leading class in capitalist Germany in the economic sense.

We can only answer the question of whether fascism corresponded to the interests of German monopoly capital by analysing the economic and social situation in Germany during the fascist period and after. If it furthered economic development, if it helped the country to extricate itself from the total social crisis which followed the end of the period of extensive economic growth, then the answer must be that it undoubtedly served the interests of German monopoly capital, since fascist rule left the foundations of property relations intact. Even in its original form, the somewhat nebulous anti-capitalism of the nazi movement was not directed towards the real transformation of property relations. If we discount the Strasser group (which lost its initially strong influence within the party), the radical phrases against international "Jewish" capital were always linked with support for "productive" capital. They reflected the unrealistic initiatives of the petty bourgeoisie and by no means embraced the idea of a radical transformation of the existing property relations; even the restriction of these relations was but barely implied. And practically nothing was done in this respect. The "restriction" of certain capitalist interests, if it was carried out, meant simply the regulation of capitalist competition by the state, which was in any case the international tendency of capitalist development and the explicit objective of German monopoly capital's leading circles.

Under a fascist dictatorship, just as under the manipulatory economy of the modern welfare state, state intervention in the economy may occur in two ways. It can take place through agreements between the executive power and the associations of capitalists (the representative organisations of the most influential capitalist circles). Or it can occur in such a way that the executive power puts through its measures and generally determines state economic policy in opposition to the capitalists and their organisations.

The first three years of the nazi régime, when the crisis was being overcome, were broadly characterised by the first of these forms. But from 1936 onwards, the second form of state intervention gained predominance. It was *against* the will of the leading circles in the traditional branches of German industry that the nazi state not only continued its rearmament policy (which until that point had had the consent and assistance of the leading capitalist circles) but resorted thereby to such a restructuring of the economy that it became not just possible but necessary — a question of life and death — for Germany to launch an expressly predatory war (and the word "predatory" must be understood here in its strictest sense).*

---

*The majority of historical works which examine the relationship be-

In the 1933-36 period the political objectives of fascism and the basic interests of the German capitalist economy practically coincided. And no one can deny that from the very beginning Hitler wove definite plans of war, and that he intended to influence the development of German industry accordingly. In the initial stages following the seizure of power there were fitful periods when the régime proclaimed to the world its peaceful intentions, but these always had expressly tactical causes. Even the least aggressive circles of the German bourgeoisie could be satisfied with the initial economic consequences of these warlike intentions, for at the time they simply meant first of all the development of the Reichswehr in violation of the Versailles treaty (but within the limits necessary for achieving normal defence strength — this was, of course, received with approval by the German economic leaders), and secondly the development of the war industry to its "normal" level, which contributed substantially to overcoming the economic crisis. It is true that in 1933 state-financed construction projects aimed at getting rid of unemployment played a bigger part in starting the industrial upswing than did the growth of production in the war industries as such. But the great state projects, especially the building of the autobahns, were just as necessary for the war preparations as were the development of the war industry itself and the build-up of the Reichswehr.

Hitler and the nazi leadership were meanwhile only interested in two things. One was to improve the social situation of the masses quickly and spectacularly (this could only be done by

---

tween the German economy and politics date this change at 1936. The importance ascribed to it by the various historians naturally depends on their theoretical attitude. My own views are based mainly on the two following marxist essays: Dieter Grosser, "Die national-sozialistische Wirtschaft", *Das Argument*, no. 1, 1965 (second edition, 1967), and Tim Mason, "The Primacy of Politics — Politics and Economics in National Socialist Germany" in S. J. Woolf (ed.), *The Nature of Fascism* (London, 1969). These essays are much more than simple descriptions of the facts about the history of fascism, about its economic history and the problem of the relationship between politics and the economy under fascism. They are in themselves important contributions to the elaboration of a marxist theory of fascism.

guaranteeing full employment), in order to maintain and broaden the régime's mass support. The other was to enhance the country's military strength. The nazi politicians were not in the least interested in how the economy was to achieve this, nor whether it was rational to expect it to happen. But these demands of the nazi politicians coincided *unequivocally* with the interests of capitalist development.

Hjalmar Schacht, the all-powerful economic "Führer" of the 1933-36 period, was the representative of the German financial bourgeoisie. I have already indicated that I disagree with the answer which Pál Justus gives to the question, why did the anti-capitalist slogans of fascism not frighten the haute bourgeoisie? He maintains that the contrast between "extorting" [*raffendes*] capital and "productive" [*schaffendes*] capital in fascist theory expressed the struggle between financial and industrial capital, and that fascism did in fact correspond to the interests of industrial capital as against those of finance capital. But quite apart from the fact that such a rigid opposition between these two strata has no factual basis, Schacht's role itself proves that finance capital, at least in the period up to the seizure of power, stood to benefit from helping the nazis to power by at least as much as the industrial bourgeoisie did. Until 1936 the *whole* of the haute bourgeoisie was satisfied with the results, and we shall see later that the *political* eclipse of the bourgeoisie after the 1936 turning-point did not result from the specific situation of the financial bourgeoisie either.

In the books[75] which Schacht wrote after the war (they were mainly intended to exculpate himself), he tried to prove that the measures he introduced would not necessarily have led to a war economy, but constituted the indispensable conditions for the peaceful stabilisation of the German capitalist economy. In this respect we can take him at his word. According to Schacht, Hitler gave no indication of his intention to prepare for war at this point, and no preparations had actually started yet. This is not true, of course, but it is not specially interesting. What is true is that his economic measures — the energetic state intervention in the workings of the capitalist economy — meant not only the first steps in a transition to a war economy, but also the first measures of a guided capitalist economy corresponding to the intensive stage of capitalist development. It is not simply (or rather not primarily)

Schacht's account which proves this. What does prove it is the essential similarity between Schacht's measures and Roosevelt's. The key problem in overcoming the crisis is getting rid of unemployment, i.e. re-starting production, and this demands the creation of effective demand for the goods produced. Both Roosevelt in the USA and Schacht in Germany achieved this (or, to be more precise, provided the initial impetus for it) partly by making state investments and partly by granting substantial credit to private capitalist enterprises. So the changes through which the crisis was surmounted came first of all in financial policy. Nevertheless, they were not simply temporary. By means of their introduction, the relationship between the capitalist economy and the state changed once and for all.

Schacht's description of what was new about his financial policy can be applied, almost word for word, to the New Deal:

> "Until then, the task of the Central Bank had been to adapt itself to the processes of the economy. If the economy was active with a big turnover and needed a lot of money, then the Central Bank issued money. When there was a recession in the economy, the Central Bank pulled money in. It used to accompany the economy, but now it had become its governor. While it had until then issued money on the already available goods to be put in circulation, it now had to issue money on goods which would become saleable only in the future."[76]

Until then it had been the untouchable taboo of state financial policy "not to issue more money than the quantity of goods already produced". This taboo was dropped by every capitalist state. But this kind of "inflationary" policy does not merely demand financial intervention by the state. It requires very severe measures to restrict the automatic operation of the capitalist economy. Unless the use of the credits issued is strictly supervised, and unless the state intervenes energetically in foreign trade and currency exchange etc., then issuing money without coverage will lead to inflation. This was characteristic of both these "experiments" — of the New Deal as well as of nazi economic policy. And it is equally the case that in Germany (as opposed to the USA, where the already-elected president held all the necessary power) the Weimar régime was incapable of guaranteeing the conditions which were essential if such an economy was to work.

However, the leading capitalist circles had no influence on the formation of policy as a whole, even in the period between 1933 and 1936. The key political positions were occupied by nazi leaders who had no close connection with the haute bourgeoisie. Schacht held key positions in economic policy, but had no voice in the country's domestic and foreign policies. But the capitalist circles were content with this situation. Everything that happened up to 1936 tallied perfectly with their interests.

The *Erbhofgesetz* (the law on land inheritance), which was designed to solve the problems of agriculture and above all those of the peasantry, was also issued in the pre-1936 period — in fact it came as early as the autumn of 1933. Here, too, the state intervened resolutely in the free development of the economy. But this measure indicated that the German economy was already being geared to the demands of imperialist expansion. It was the first measure to reveal clearly how the fascist state gave priority to political requirements over economic ones. By protecting the holdings of the small and middle peasant proprietors and by putting an end to their uncertainty about their own existence, the *Erbhofgesetz* drove all the young peasants out of agriculture (except for eldest sons). As full employment was secured, so this offered the possibility of work even to them. But their problems could not really be solved in this way, nor would they have accepted this solution on a mass scale (and it was not even promised them). It was from this stratum that the SS was recruited; its members were selected to become the owners of the Slav land that would be conquered. This created not just a human resource for the war of conquest in general, but one of the goals for the war itself, i.e. the extermination or enslavement of the original population of the territories to be conquered. Thus the solution of the agrarian problem in 1933 already pointed to the coming period, without adversely affecting the interests of the haute bourgeoisie in the least (even the interests of the Prussian Junkers were respected: the large estates were not touched at all).

By 1936 all the basic economic problems which had appeared almost insoluble at the time of the nazis' seizure of power were solved, and Germany could have joined the trend of normal economic development. But this would have required two things.

114

The first was that the country should join in normal world trade. In the case of Germany, which was poor in raw materials, this meant exporting its industrial products in order to buy the indispensable raw materials in exchange. The second was that the population should be able to satisfy its needs to a *permanently* increasing extent, thereby securing a growing market for the developing economy. However, as opposed to the New Deal, the Third Reich's "new order" left no room for these preconditions to be met.

As far as these basic aspects of economic policy are concerned, the German and American experiments chose exactly opposite solutions. The re-starting of the economy presupposes that the goods produced should meet with demand. At the beginning, the growth in demand in both countries was secured by the considerable reduction of unemployment (which was achieved by "artificial" means for the first time in the history of capitalism). Because unemployment was reduced much more quickly in Germany than in the USA (by the end of 1933 it was already cut by a third), effective demand there increased rapidly for three or four years without making any rise in the real wages of the workers necessary. (The respective data are in fact very contradictory. According to some, real wages increased in the 1933-36 period; according to others, real wages were already falling then, and not only during the war period. This is not the point, however, for the fascist corporations did not exist to safeguard the workers' interests and they did not perform the functions which trade unions do in neo-capitalism.) Once Germany had achieved full employment, the developing industries could only secure a market by switching decisively over to war production. In the USA one of the basic features of the New Deal was the introduction of welfare measures which secured the livelihoods of the most diverse social strata by means of state support (old age pensions, for example); the other, even more important aspect of this was the political support which the régime gave to the reformist trade unions (it was Roosevelt who made the rights of American trade unions really effective). As a result of this, the demand for the goods produced became permanent. Nazism, on the other hand, abolished all the organisations which safeguarded working-class interests, and so there was nothing to force the individual capitalist into raising his employees' wages.

In 1936, therefore, at a time when full employment had practically been achieved, German economic policy (or to be more exact, industrial policy) was confronted with a fateful choice. One alternative was to keep the rate of armaments at a "normal" level (the army was already equipped at a "normal" level, according to the defence requirements of the period), and to switch industry over to the production of consumer goods, providing investment for peaceful production. Industry would become competitive in export markets and the demand for imported goods would not rise enough to upset the balance of trade.

The other alternative was to increase armaments production at an accelerated rate.

Schacht, who represented German monopoly capital and especially its leading wing, the iron and steel industry, opted for the first of these solutions. The leading bourgeois circles had certainly not taken all the consequences of such a choice into account. One of these was that the social provisions of the New Deal would have to be imitated too: their members would have to renounce a substantial part of their profits for the sake of satisfying the population's ever-increasing demands. But even if they had been aware of this, it would still have been in their interests to choose the peaceful solution. It was true that the big capitalists in the USA were forced to give up a substantial part of their individual profit for the sake of their employees, and that the emerging nazi economy did not force the German capitalists to act in a similar way. Nevertheless, the American method was a sure way out of the crisis of liberal capitalism (and the fundamental interest of the capitalist class as a class was to find this way out), whereas the fascist road could only be, necessarily, a temporary one.

On the other hand, however, the nazi leaders themselves had only one choice: to develop the war industries. Why?

We can accept no argument that refers to ideological causes — to the anti-Soviet attitude of Hitler and his group, to Hitler's personal aspirations in the field of world politics etc. This would be to locate the causes of events in the fanaticism of a few people or a movement; it does not take into account the ease with which Hitler himself and almost all the members of his leading clique threw away their convictions whenever their interests demanded it. And while it is true that none of the nazi leaders was a qualified expert in economic affairs, it would be absurd to paint them

116

as imbeciles unable to understand the convincing arguments of the economic experts and the truth of those arguments. To see the nazis as ordinary imbeciles is to forget what brilliant politicians they proved to be during the period just before and after the seizure of power, when they got rid of all their opponents with incredible rapidity. And it is childish, too, to maintain that after 1936 they became intoxicated with their successes and from then on believed they would succeed in anything they did. It is not only more convincing but also much easier to explain Hitler's post-1936 decisions in terms of the interests of the nazi clique.

What would it have meant to the nazi régime in 1936 if the Germany economy had joined in with peaceful world trade and if the policy had been to raise the standard of living? It would have meant, quite definitely, that they had accomplished their historical mission. What excuse could there have been for preserving a totalitarian dictatorship in circumstances where the economy was geared to satisfying the material needs of the broad masses of the population, when there was no longer any unemployment and the standard of living kept on rising? It would have been much more suitable for the bourgeoisie to return to the parliamentary system; with the roots of fascism as a *mass movement* undercut in this way, there would have been no force for the nazi clique to defend itself with. I am convinced that if the material needs of the broadest layers of the population had been satisfied, then German nationalism and the feelings of humiliation and offence (which undoubtedly existed) at the conditions of the Versailles treaty would not have been enough to keep the nazi movement in existence. It was in the nazis' vital interests to keep the tension up artificially, and to create a situation of no return. For them, the loss of political power would have meant their complete disappearance. By 1936 the leading nazi élite had still not been integrated into the economic ruling class and had gained no economic power. They could not have retired from politics like ordinary bourgeois without impairing their own material interests.

The armament and war preparations policies meant that even with full employment the population's living standards could be kept at a low level and the source of tension maintained — a tension which in the eyes of the masses (the nazis "proved" this to them) could only be solved by war. The internal dynamic of the nazi régime necessarily led it towards war and accelerated armaments production, and the system was capable of realising this internal tendency even when, from the point of view of monopoly capital, it had already fulfilled its "historical mission".

What were the results of this changeover to war production? The war industries produced unsaleable commodities, or to be more precise, commodities which only the state could purchase. Consequently the state got into debt (Schacht clearly perceived the historical moment after which it was catastrophe to continue the inflationary policy), and the economy was unable to import the raw materials which were indispensable for the development of the war industry itself. In order to avoid the ensuing vicious circle, in which the very development of the war industry became the main obstacle to its further development, Germany had to produce, *at any price*, the required goods (and above all rubber) from the raw materials at its disposal. Tim Mason writes: "If rearmament was not to be scaled down, the only way to avoid a repetition of the foreign trade crisis of 1936 was to bring about an immense increase in the domestic production of raw materials."[77] But the enforced intensification of raw materials production further increased the national debt. The state was prepared to pay the synthetics industry any price for substitutes for the missing raw materials: thus the armaments policy demanded the forced development of new branches in the chemical industry. But it did not only do this. It also demanded the uneconomical production of traditional raw materials. The raw material requirements of the war industry had to be met to the greatest possible extent from internal resources, since the inability to export resulted in a currency deficit. So, for example, the nazis demanded that a type of iron ore be used which made the price of the crude iron thus produced several times higher than the world market price. The Hermann Göring Werke were originally set up to process this economically unexploitable iron ore.

Göring, who followed Hjalmar Schacht as Führer of the economy though he was a complete layman on economic questions, followed a policy of consistent and exclusive attention to the requirements of war preparations. The requirements of economic rationality were abolished.

Why did the leading circles of the bourgeoisie accept this policy? It could be argued, for example, that individual capitalists could not have been forced to "choose" the other, American way, even if in historical perspective this tallied with the class interests of the bourgeoisie; individual capitalists naturally prefer (except in crisis situations) their own private interests to the general interest of the capitalist class as such, and Roosevelt himself only succeeded after meeting great difficulties. But in Germany the situation was radically different. In the 1933-36 period the monopoly capitalist circles intervened only in economic and social policy, and surrendered all the key positions in internal and foreign politics to the nazis, who by 1936 were already in a position to oppose them in the sphere of economic policy too. Because it had voluntarily withdrawn from politics during the first years of nazi power, it later lost even the ability to intervene. In 1936 it no longer had any effective means of opposing those who held executive power, and whose popularity had even increased since 1933 as a result of their successes in economic policy. An important part was also played by the fact that the Reichswehr, which had been neutral and weak in 1933, was already strong by 1936, and a considerable number of its leaders were friendly to the nazis. Consequently the bourgeoisie acquiesced in the régime's armaments policy, which went beyond the point of no return. The catastrophic nature of this policy was clear to the bourgeoisie, who realised that the rapid rate of armaments production might force war to break out before victory could be guaranteed (and this is what actually happened). But it acquiesced all the more because this policy directly corresponded with its material interests, at least as far as the biggest industrial sectors were concerned.

From this point on there could be no question of the bourgeoisie as a class being able to represent its own interests directly. The economic decisions were in the hands of the nazi leaders, and the state became the principal, almost exclusive customer. As a result, competition between the various capitalist groups intensified — not for the free market (which was very restricted) but for state orders. The losers were those groups which were unable to switch over to war production, and that meant the capitalists in the consumer goods industries. All those who obtained orders from the state received gigantic profits, since the state was, as we have seen, prepared to pay any price in order to increase the rate of armaments production. Naturally, it was the new branches of the chemical industry that scooped the largest profits, and as a result of this an important change came about in the relationship among the various capitalist interests. Whereas before the nazi seizure of power the iron and steel industry had been the leading stratum of German capital, from 1933 onwards the chemical industry was equally important. The nazi programme, therefore, brought about significant changes in the structure of German industry. And these changes contributed to the fact that today Germany is in economic terms the leading capitalist country in Europe. In Dieter Grosser's words, "The economic power of many large enterprises in the Federal Republic has its roots in the period of armaments and the war economy."[78]

Thus even if there were some capitalist circles whose direct material interests lost out as a result of the nazi régime's unbridled armaments policy, this policy did not hinder the immediate interests of the bourgeoisie's main sectors. Their incomes increased substantially. Grosser has shown that after 1936 industrial income increased to a much greater degree than the national income or the incomes of employees did.[79] The bourgeoisie willingly gave up intervening in politics because the loss of its political power was accompanied by a huge increase in its economic power, and in any case every single capitalist or group of capitalists remained omnipotent within the domain of the enterprise and of the economy itself. But the general interests of aggregate capital were not asserted or realised. To be more precise, the operative mechanism of the economy in the nazi period did not historically constitute a structure meeting the basic collective interests of the bourgeoisie — i.e. it did not correspond to the model of the stable mechanism in the intensive period of development. The interests that could be realised within the framework of this economy were, besides those of the group which held political power, the interests of partial groups of capitalists who competed against each other more fiercely than ever before. In Tim Mason's words:

> "This intensification and change in the character of capitalist competition contributed further to the disintegration of the political power of industry in general. . . . The collective interest of the capitalistic economic system dissolved progressively from 1936 to 1939 into a mere agglomeration of the short-term interests of individual firms."[80]

The state intervention policy played a more significant role in the fascist régime than in modern, manipulative capitalism. But while in the latter case state intervention essentially means balancing and reconciling the conflictive interests of particular capitalist groups for the sake of the general interest of the whole bourgeoisie, the intervention of the fascist state in the economy was different. Fascist policies were not determined by the economic sphere's interest in reconciling private capitalist interests: they were based precisely on the exploitation of the antagonisms among these private capitalists. The fascist régime asserted the political interests of the leading nazi stratum in such a way that in the economic sphere it promoted the natural play of capitalist competition in an intensified form. Paradoxically, then, a situation arose where the monopoly capitalist government of the USA restricted the individual capitalist in the realisation of his everyday interests much more than the fascist régime did, whose members were more independent of the big capitalists. But precisely because of this, the American New Deal represented the historical interests of the bourgeoisie as a class much more clearly than fascism did. In serving the everyday capitalist interests and thus taking the road to ruin, fascism mainly represented the power interests of the ruling political group.

The turning-point of 1936 was determined purely by the political interests of the political leadership. Tim Mason has rightly maintained that the relationship thus brought about between politics and the economy was unique in the history of capitalism. *The absolute primacy of politics over the total interests of the economy was established.* We have seen that the establishment of this primacy was made a great deal easier by the fact that the kind of politics involved decisively promoted the realisation of private economic interests. Or to be more precise, it was able to hinder the realisation of the bourgeoisie's collective interest because at the same time it gave quite important sectors of the bourgeoisie the chance to make unprecedented profits.

The "primacy of politics" did not mean, however, that it had to impress its requirements on the economy by the constant use of force. The turning-point meant such a readjustment in the economy itself that, once it had happened, its own self-movement was already driving it to satisfy the requirements of politics. Angelo Tasca, writing in 1936, made the following remarks (calling the economic system which had been established "the fascist economy", perhaps with some exaggeration):

"The fascist economy is a 'planned and closed' one directed towards war. Production costs, competition [true for the national economy, but not for individual private enterprises — M.V.], and even profit itself have in general no decisive function in it. The political goal of preparing for war stands above all economic considerations, and the resulting organisation of the economy cannot for its part serve any other goal but this one. . . . In fascism the state does not simply replace the private capitalist as the organiser of the economy, but also forces its own political plans as a priority on the private capitalist. The proper domain of fascism is power, not profit."[81]

Even though I cannot agree with such a rigid counterposing of power and profit (as we have seen, the sanctity of profit was preserved intact), I think that Tasca formulated a very important idea: the organisation of the economy itself is transformed in the course of time in such as way that it *cannot* serve any other purpose.

The wasteful form of management of resources which was introduced in 1936 completely ignored the requirements of economic rationality, and as a result the national debt increased to a staggering extent. It created a situation in the German national economy from which the only way out was a predatory war that would refloat the economy by means — literally — of robbery and slave labour. The form of economic management introduced in 1936 made the war mandatory, and made it directly necessary to loot the occupied territories, to displace and enslave their populations without giving them even the barest necessities of existence.

Not even the most brutal and genocidal measures of the nazi régime need be put down to the sadism or "madness" of its leaders. A régime had been born which needed these measures in order to survive. The "normal" wars of history and the normal wars of bourgeois society have almost always been started in order to achieve some concrete objective. It follows from the nature of the fascist régime that the objective of this war was not and could not have been anything but the war itself.

In order to commit those dreadful atrocities, which were

122

unprecedented in history and were the necessary consequence of the nature of the régime itself, some ideological "basis" was needed. One cannot exterminate millions of people in the name of economic interests or of the power interests of a clique. Those who were enslaved, exploited to the very last of their working ability and then destroyed, had to be "proved" inferior or even completely non-human. The Prussian principle of "following orders" could not alone have forced hundreds of thousands of people to become sadistic mass murderers. Since the basis was an apparently ideological one, it was unavoidable that in the last resort certain very rational crimes should have been accompanied, not only apparently but actually, by irrational atrocities too. If the Jews and the occupied peoples were to be deported not because the nazi clique had to continue the ruthless exploitation of the economy and the predatory war for the sake of maintaining their own rule, but because they had to prevent the proliferation of inferior races, then it followed that those who had no usable working capacity should be deported too. If such actions served "higher goals", then sometimes they had to be carried out against all sober considerations. If the SS was brought up to wipe its victims out because they were not human beings, then there was no basis of rational argument for stopping their extermination even when it needed to be stopped. If the extermination of people serves objectives "of a higher order", then it cannot be stopped for the sake of "low" material interests.

There are many examples to demonstrate the way in which this irrationality surfaced. When German industry needed to use the work of the excellent Polish skilled workers in crafts where they would be required to pay them a normal wage (even though this would have been less than the German workers' wage) and to treat them as "free" people (if such a word can be used about the Third Reich), the SS resisted. And thousands of Polish skilled workers whom German industry urgently needed were deported, made to work as slaves and in the end killed. To take another example, the German army had serious supply difficulties during the last year of the war, and "rationality" seemed to demand that all railway lines and locomotives should be used to service the front. They were used instead to transport Jews from nearly all the European countries into the extermination camps, including millions who were immediately gassed because it would not have been "economic" to let them work even as slaves.

Thus the ideology which served the rational objectives of the régime undoubtedly became irrational in many cases, and worked against its "vital interests". But this in the last resort simply expressed and made visible the fundamental irrationality of the régime as a whole. I am in full agreement with Tim Mason:

"Under the conditions of capitalist production, there is always something irrational about the assertion of a primacy of politics, since that which alone can legitimate this primacy, a commonweal, can only be simulated."[82]

Rendering the state completely independent (which is a characteristic of fascism) meant *of necessity* that the régime would destroy itself. This was not because the executive power came into conflict with capitalist interests, but because it freed the principle of capitalist competition from all institutional restraints. Executive power served the political interests of a ruling clique which set aside all the dictates of rationality; it simultaneously served those private capitalist interests which emerged from competition with success. This latter circumstance points beyond the downfall of the fascist system. From the economic point of view, the spectacular defeat of Germany in the second world war was only the defeat of the leading nazi stratum, not of German monopoly capital. The German "economic miracle" owes its existence to the fact that nazi economic policy ignored the dictates of "reason", not to the Marshall Plan.

Was the German ruling class transformed during the nazi period, did the class structure change? The marxist interpreters of fascism have provided diametrically opposite answers to this question. Both the official Comintern analysts and many noncommunist marxists answered it in the negative. In addition, they both denied that fascism represented the interests of anyone but the haute bourgeoisie. Otto Bauer for example, who as we have seen laid great emphasis on the petty bourgeois origins of the fascist movement, asserted that "even if the fascist dictatorship sprang from a balance of class forces, its establishment and stabilisation put an end to this balance".[83] With this I agree. But he also drew the conclusion:

"The leading stratum of the bourgeoisie, the representatives of monopoly capital and of the large estates succeeded with extraordinary rapidity after the establishment of the fascist dictatorship in turning the new régime into a tool of their class rule, and in transforming the new masters into their servants. . . . Even if the fascist dictatorship rules over the capitalist class, it nevertheless inevitably becomes the executive organ of the needs, interests and *will* of the capitalist class [my italics — M.V.]."[84]

I regard this view of Bauer's as untenable. How can a régime carry out the will of a class if it rules over that class? How can a power system rule over those whom it actually serves? "Needs", "interests" and "will" cannot automatically be considered as identical. I have tried to make it clear that while fascism corresponded in many ways to the interests of the haute bourgeoisie, it did not correspond to its will. Bauer's viewpoint, as well as the official Comintern one, sets out from an oversimplified schema of the relation between rule and power. This is equally typical of both the social democratic and stalinist schools of marxism. It presupposes that economic power *automatically* grants to a class the possession of political rule too, that the representation of a class's interests can only be carried out in one way, and that this way is somehow or other automatically willed by the class in question. The class relations (or to be more precise, the relations of class affiliation) are reduced to one single factor — that of the legal possession of the means of production — and all other factors, particularly the question of who controls the relations of production, are considered secondary.

The opposite view, however, is no less a simplification. When Angelo Tasca,[85] for example, asserts that the fascist bureaucracy and ruling clique form a new class — a class which does not occupy a definite position in the economy but with which the bourgeoisie has to compromise — then he is overlooking the fact that the beneficiaries of a régime do not necessarily form a class, precisely because they have no guarantee of their economic privileges once they have lost their political power. If a social stratum enjoys material privileges solely because it possesses political power, then it cannot be considered a class.

Our analysis implies that although the fascist dictatorship corresponded to the direct material interests of the bourgeoisie, in many ways it also came into conflict with certain bourgeois interests, governing against the will of the bourgeoisie and in the interests of a stratum whose political power allowed it to obtain

125

material advantages within the framework of the given régime. Consequently it is not true that fascist dictatorship only served the interests of the haute bourgeoisie or of the ruling classes generally, nor is it true that it served these interests unequivocally and in all respects. But the social advantages enjoyed by those beneficiaries of the régime who did not belong to the leading economic classes were bound to its political form; therefore, although the fascist leadership did not belong to the bourgeoisie, it did not form a new class either. This cannot be argued against by saying that the fascist leadership possessed economic power. It undeniably had such power — not within the capitalist factory but certainly at the level of the national economy. Because of the structure of the régime, its leading political role enabled it to guide the economy (in this respect the fascist version of the "Tenth of December Society" played an entirely different role from that of Bonaparte's Society). This, however, does not contradict what I said about the fascist leadership not being a class, for the fascists' economic power did not spring from the normal functioning of the economic system as governed by its own autonomous laws, but from their own political role. When they lost their political power, the economy automatically switched to a course which really did correspond to the requirements of the intensive phase of development, and this automatically meant the end of the fascist leaders' economic power too.

The question is complicated by one specific point. The fascist leaders, or many of them, seized huge amounts of private property and amassed a considerable amount of capital, inheritable capital. I am not speaking about Göring, who was an exceptional case: he became the owner of one of the biggest enterprises in Germany, but he could only remain owner as long as he was one of the régime's leading figures. I am speaking about the accumulation of wealth of an expressly private nature. Some of this property remained in the possession of the former nazi leaders even after the downfall of the régime. But this does not prove that a new class had arisen. If the nazi leaders had become owners of major capitalist enterprises, then they would simply have become capitalists, and would thus have been personally integrated into the original capitalist class. Since membership of the bourgeoisie has never been a "naturally given" condition in the way that the class affiliations of previous societies were, this is an everyday occurrence in capitalist societies and does not point to the rise of a new class.

There is, then, no reason for me to alter what I said. The other beneficiary of the régime apart from the haute bourgeoisie was the stratum which held political power. But its benefits were tied to its political power, and our description of the "peculiar nature" of "classical" fascism is based on this.

Nazism drove nearly the whole of mankind into the biggest war in history, a war which demanded terrifying sacrifices. The loss of the war meant the downfall of the régime. Nazism left the stage of history, and only its ghost reappears here and there. Nor could it have survived. Its existence had to be temporary. The crisis of the social system which had been adequate to the phase of extensive capitalist development did not demand the appearance of fascism as even a temporary necessity: fascism happened because this crisis coincided with the quite specific political situation of Germany.

This thesis needs, however, to be backed up from another angle. It calls for an investigation of why the fascistoid movements did not achieve any serious success in the other developed capitalist countries: for even if it was unable to obtain a real mass effect elsewhere, it certainly existed outside Italy and Germany. Why is this a problem of fundamental importance? Because it is questionable whether the Western capitalist countries would have been able to switch over to a neo-capitalist system with democratic forms if fascism had not been victorious in Germany. The victory of the fascist movement in Germany, the aggressiveness which it made abundantly obvious from the beginning, and its launching of the second world war: all these things undeniably contributed to the success of the New Deal and to the ability of the West European capitalist countries to extricate themselves from the crisis. Germany forced them to switch over to a war economy. It would, of course, be unhistorical and senseless to ask what would have happened if German history had not taken this turn. But we might view fascism in a different light if we tried to answer the following questions.

What part did the world war, which was initiated by nazi Germany, play in the evolution of the modern neo-capitalist system? And how far did the world war help the entire capitalist world to set up the social structure which corresponds to this new phase of economic development?

NOTES

1. See the section entitled "Class Consciousness" in Georg Lukács, *History and Class Consciousness* (London, 1971).
2. Otto Bauer, "Der Faschismus" in Bauer, Marcuse, Rosenberg *et al.*, *Faschismus und Kapitalismus* (Frankfurt and Vienna, 1967), p. 143.
3. Herbert Marcuse, "The Struggle against Liberalism in the Totalitarian View of the State" in *Negations* (London, 1968), p. 17.
4. *Ibid.*
5. See the section entitled "Reification and the Consciousness of the Proletariat" in Georg Lukács, *History and Class Consciousness.*
6. Marcuse, *op. cit.*, p. 16.
7. *Ibid.*, p. 17.
8. *Ibid.*
9. *Ibid.*, p. 18.
10. *Ibid.*, p. 19.
11. *Ibid.*, p. 21.
12. Karl Marx, "On the Jewish Question" in Karl Marx and Frederick Engels, *Collected Works* (London and Moscow, 1975), vol. 3, p. 164.
13. *Ibid.*, p. 153.
14. *Ibid.*, p. 156.
15. *Ibid.*, p. 155.
16. Antonio Gramsci, "Die italienische Krise" in *Philosophie der Praxis* (Frankfurt, 1967), p. 378. Translated from German.
17. Agnes Heller, *A mindennapi élet* (Budapest, 1970). German translation, *Alltag und Geschichte* (Neuwied, 1970).
18. See C. M. Gilbert, *Nuremburg Diary.*
19. Georg Lukács, in *Schriften zur Ideologie und Politik* (Neuwied, 1967).
20. Erich Fromm, *The Fear of Freedom* (London, 1942).
21. *Ibid.*
22. Gramsci, "Arbeiter und Bauer" in *op. cit.*, p. 38.
23. *Ibid.*, p. 100.
24. *Ibid.*, p. 109.
25. *Ibid.*, p. 153.
26. Angelo Tasca (*pseud.* A. Rossi), *The Rise of Italian Fascism* (London, 1938).
27. See *ibid.*, p. 343.
28. *Ibid.*, pp. 344-5.
29. See *ibid.*, pp. 350-1.

30. Hermann Heller, *Europa und der Faschimus* (1929).
31. *Ibid.*, p. 17.
32. *Ibid.*, p. 16.
33. *Ibid.*, p. 20.
34. *Ibid.*, p. 23.
35. *Ibid.*, p. 40.
36. *Ibid.*, p. 10.
37. Leon Trotsky, "What Next?" in Trotsky, *Germany 1931-2* (London, 1970), p. 69.
38. See Karl Korsch, "The Fascist Counter-Revolution" in *Living Marxism*, vol. 5, no. 2 (1940), p. 33.
39. *Ibid.*, p. 34.
40. See Gunnar Myrdal, "Beyond the Welfare State" in *Economic Planning in the Welfare States and its International Implications* (London, 1960).
41. Franz Borkenau, "Zur Soziologie des Faschimus" in *Archiv für Sozialwissenschaften und Sozialpolitik* (Tubingen, 1933), pp. 513-47.
42. Gramsci, "Ein Jahr" in *op. cit.*, p. 102.
43. *Ibid.*, p. 105.
44. Borkenau, *op. cit.*, p. 525.
45. Trotsky, *op. cit.*, pp. 64-5 and 69.
46. Trotsky, *The Turn in the Communist International and the German Situation* (New York, 1930).
47. Bauer, *op. cit.*, p. 154.
48. Ignazio Silone, *Der Faschimus* (Zürich, 1934), pp. 70 and 71.
49. Marx, "The Eighteenth Brumaire of Louis Bonaparte" in Karl Marx, *Selected Works* (Moscow, 1936), vol. 2, p. 325.
50. Lukács, *op. cit.*, pp. 310-11.
51. *Ibid.*, pp. 312-13.
52. Quoted in Bauer, *op. cit.*, p. 5.
53. Hermann Heller, *op. cit.*, p. 123.
54. Iring Fetscher, "Zur Kritik des sowjetmarxistischen Faschismusbegriffs" in *Karl Marx und der Marxismus* (Munich, 1967), p. 237.
55. August Thalheimer, "Uber den Faschismus" in Bauer, *op. cit.*, p. 28.
56. Tasca, *op. cit.*, p. 338.
57. Marx, *op. cit.*, p. 383.
58. *Ibid.*, p. 396.
59. *Ibid.*, p. 346.
60. *Ibid.*, p. 362.
61. Letter from Engels to Marx on 13 April 1866, in *Marx-Engels Selected Correspondence* (Moscow, 1955), p. 177.

62. Marx, *op. cit.*, pp. 371-2.
63. *Ibid.*, p. 379.
64. *Ibid.*, p. 420.
65. *Ibid.*, p. 423-4.
66. *Ibid.*, p. 414.
67. *Ibid.*
68. *Ibid.*, p. 415.
69. *Ibid.*
70. See for example Theo Pirker, "Vorbemerkung" in *Im Komintern und Faschimus. Dokumente zur Geschichte und Theorie des Faschismus* (Stuttgart, 1965), p. 21.
71. Marx, *op. cit.*, pp. 385-6.
72. R. Griepenburg and K. H. Tjaden, "Faschismus und Bonapartismus" in *Das Argument*, no. 6 (1966).
73. *Ibid.*, p. 461.
74. See Daniel Lerner, *The Nazi Elite* (Stanford, 1951).
75. Hjalmar Schacht, *Abrechnung mit Hitler* (Hamburg, 1948), and *1933: Wie eine Demokratie stirbt* (Düsseldorf, 1968).
76. *Ibid.* (1968), pp. 99-100.
77. Tim Mason, "The Primacy of Politics—Politics and Economics in National Socialist Germany" in S. J. Woolf (ed.), *The Nature of Fascism* (London, 1969), p. 178.
78. Dieter Grosser, "Die nationalsozialistische Wirtschaft" in *Das Argument*, no. 1, 1965 (second edition 1967), p. 6.
79. *Ibid.*, p. 5.
80. Mason, *op. cit.*, p. 181.
81. Tasca, *op. cit.*, p. 350.
82. Mason, *op. cit.*, p. 193.
83. Bauer, *op. cit.*, p. 156.
84. *Ibid.*, p. 157.
85. Tasca, *op. cit.*, p. 351.

INDEX OF NAMES

Some other titles in the MOTIVE series

Michel Raptis
Revolution and Counter-Revolution in Chile

Henri Lefebvre
The Survival of Capitalism

Franz Jakubowski
Ideology and Superstructure in Historical Materialism

Agnes Heller
The Theory of Need in Marx

Jiri Pelikan
Socialist Opposition in Eastern Europe

Hilda Scott
Women and Socialism — Experiences from Eastern Europe

Andras Hegedus
Socialism and Bureaucracy

Andras Hegedus, Agnes Heller, Maria Markus, Mihaly Vajda
The Humanisation of Socialism

Bill Lomax
Hungary 1956

Henri Laborit
Decoding the Human Message